ANTI-PROTECTION: CHANGING FORCES IN
UNITED STATES TRADE POLITICS

POLICY ANALYSES IN INTERNATIONAL ECONOMICS 21

ANTI-PROTECTION: CHANGING FORCES IN UNITED STATES TRADE POLITICS

I.M.Destler
John S.Odell

Assisted by
Kimberly Ann Elliott

INSTITUTE FOR INTERNATIONAL ECONOMICS
WASHINGTON, DC
SEPTEMBER 1987

I.M. Destler, a former Senior Fellow at the Institute, is now Professor of Public Affairs at the University of Maryland and a Visiting Fellow at the Institute.

John S. Odell, a Visiting Fellow at the Institute, is Associate Professor of International Relations at the University of Southern California.

Kimberly Ann Elliott is a Research Associate at the Institute.

We owe many debts. Robert Baldwin, Gary Horlick, and an anonymous third reader offered extremely helpful critiques of our penultimate draft; Marcus Noland and William R. Cline advised on data analysis. Joseph Damond and Laura Knoy provided research assistance; Grant Taylor helped develop econometric estimates. Many trade policy practitioners offered information and advice—directly, and in study group meetings. Above all, we thank C. Fred Bergsten for sponsorship and on-target advice, Cynthia Renee Ware for typing and administrative help, and Kimberly Ann Elliott whose aid on many fronts was invaluable in the study's completion.

I.M.D. *and* J.S.O.

INSTITUTE FOR INTERNATIONAL ECONOMICS
11 Dupont Circle, NW
Washington, DC 20036
(202)328–9000 Telex: 248329 CEIP Fax (202)328–5432

Library of Congress Cataloging in Publication Data

Destler, I. M.
    Anti-Protection: Changing Forces in United States Trade Politics
(Policy analyses in international economics; 21)
    1. United States—Commercial policy. 2. Free trade and protection. I. Odell, John S., 1945–
II. Title. III. Series.
HF1455. D482   1987   382'13'0973   87-22545
ISBN 0–88132–065–X

Contents

viii

Preface

Trade policy is a focal point of international economic attention in 1987 and for the foreseeable future, with new legislation under consideration in the United States Congress and the launching of the Uruguay Round of multilateral negotiations in the GATT. In an effort to contribute significantly to the debate, the Institute is simultaneously releasing studies on four major trade policy issues: agriculture, auction quotas (and the broader issue of implementing quantitative import controls), the politics of anti-protection, and textiles.

To our knowledge, this is the first study to analyze systematically the forces that oppose trade restraint. Both economists and political scientists have made a number of valuable efforts to probe "the market for protection" and the forces that promote new barriers to the international flow of commerce. But no previous analysis has sought to delineate those elements in the American body politic which have an interest in avoiding such barriers, to determine when those elements have in fact been active in the trade policy debate and why, and what impact their efforts may have had on final policy decisions. The purpose of this study is to provide a better balance in the understanding of trade politics in the United States, and to offer suggestions on how a better balance can be carried into the policy arena as well.

The Institute for International Economics is a private nonprofit research institution for the study and discussion of international economic policy. Its purpose is to analyze important issues in that area, and to develop and communicate practical new approaches for dealing with them. The Institute is completely nonpartisan.

The Institute was created by a generous commitment of funds from the German Marshall Fund of the United States in 1981, and continues to receive substantial support from that source. This study was largely financed by the J. Howard Pew Freedom Trust, whose help is deeply appreciated.

In addition, major institutional grants are now being received from the Ford Foundation, the William and Flora Hewlett Foundation, and the Alfred

P. Sloan Foundation. The Dayton Hudson Foundation provides partial support for the Institute's program of studies on trade policy. A number of other foundations and private corporations are contributing to the increasing diversification of the Institute's financial resources.

The Board of Directors bears overall responsibility for the Institute and gives general guidance and approval to its research program—including identification of topics that are likely to become important to policymakers over the medium run (generally, one to three years) and which thus should be addressed by the Institute. The Director, working closely with the staff and outside Advisory Committee, is responsible for the development of particular projects and makes the final decision to publish an individual study.

The Institute hopes that its studies and other activities will contribute to building a stronger foundation for international economic policy around the world. Comments as to how it can best do so are invited from readers of these publications.

C. FRED BERGSTEN
Director
July 1987

1 Introduction and Summary

Despite repeated public declarations to the contrary, governments in recent years have increased import barriers, especially in forms other than tariffs. Some recent restrictions are "gray area measures" well beyond internationally sanctioned forms of trade protection. Many citizens around the globe fear that this trend is causing more harm than good, and could undermine future prosperity and welfare. They are looking, therefore, for ways to point policies back in the liberal direction.

Many of the new restrictions have allowed considerable trade to keep flowing, however, and many demands for even tighter protection have been resisted. One reason why protection has not been greater is the political role played by private interests that benefit from international trade and pay a high price when it is curbed. This role is the subject of this study.

In examining the politics of anti-protection, this study does not undertake a comprehensive analysis of current trade politics, much less propose any comprehensive solution. Rather, it investigates a particular phenomenon that seems central to successful management of international trade, which nevertheless remains quite poorly understood. Political pressures in favor of new protection are widely recognized and have been studied at length in the United States and a few other countries. What has been missing is a picture of the forces that suffer from import restrictions, and the role they play or can play in trade politics.

On the conventional view, US trade policy is a running battle between "special interests" favoring protection and "the general interest" in open trade. The "losers" in international competition have their jobs hanging on the decision, while others have more diffuse interests.

Much US experience accords with this view, but something new has also been happening. Over the last decade and a half, special interests that suffer from trade restrictions have mounted more vigorous and increasingly overt political efforts to oppose campaigns for new import restrictions. "Anti-

1

protectionism'' has been on the rise. Yet we know surprisingly little about that side of the ongoing policy struggle.

The purpose of this book is to help fill that gap. It is the first attempt, to our knowledge, at a systematic investigation and analysis of anti-protection political activity in the United States. And notwithstanding this national focus, the questions we explore are of interest in many other countries as well.

Essentially they are three:

● *What has been happening?* Which groups have been more and less active on the anti-protection side of recent trade issues, and how has this changed?

● *Why?* What produces changes and variations in this activity across groups? What could cause changes in the future?

● *What difference, if any, does this activity make* in the content of US trade policy?

A necessary prelude to these questions is a fourth: *who pays for protection, and thus would be expected to act politically?* Which are the interests within the American economy that depend on international trade and suffer most directly from its restriction?

The primary empirical basis for our analysis is 14 episodes in recent US trade policy, occasions when specific producers sought protection from imports. Since product-specific initiatives are only part of the drama of American trade politics, however, we have supplemented this with a brief examination of the political process concerning changes in generic trade law.

This introductory chapter outlines our four main arguments. The body of our study develops them and other arguments with evidence and some qualifications. The last chapter draws out implications for persons who are concerned about the apparently rising global movement toward trade protection.

(1) Restrictions on a given imported product bear more directly on certain groups than on others. *Among those who pay for protection, those who matter most in the political process are not* household consumers but the *special interests that benefit most from the specific trade that would be restricted: industrial users* of imports, *retailers* of traded consumer goods, US *exporters* who sell to the countries whose goods would be restricted, and the *companies and governments of those countries.* (This point is developed in chapter 3.)

(2) *There was a sharp increase in aggregate political opposition to product-specific trade protection over the decade from the mid-1970s to the mid-1980s.* (This argument is found mostly in chapter 3, with documentation in appendix A.) Activity in reaction to proposed increases in import protection varied greatly from group to group and from one product episode to the next, ranging from mere letter writing to massive, expensive campaigns, involving widespread lobbying in Washington, thousands of constituent letters, and overseas threats of retaliation. Several types of groups were particularly active: highly dependent exporters, highly dependent import-using industries, retailers (when a consumer good was at issue), and governments and companies of targeted exporting countries. Multinational companies, banks, and broad commercial organizations like the Chamber of Commerce typically avoided involvement in product-specific protection battles. Most consumer organizations avoided making major or even minor commitments in international trade politics.

It is also true that the increased opposition in product cases was mostly reactive and episodic, and was still not as great as might have been expected on economic grounds, at least on first glance. And it certainly did not defeat all pro-protection campaigns. Nevertheless, the anti-protection phenomenon grew substantially in response to proposed increases in restrictions of auto, copper, footwear, steel, sugar, and textile imports. Our data also suggest that, among anti-protection interests, activity by import-related groups was rising sharply in the 1980s, whereas activity by export-related ones was flat or falling—at least in relative terms.

There does not appear to have been a comparable increase in opposition to generic trade-restrictive proposals, such as amendments to trade remedy laws aimed at increasing their utility to firms seeking trade relief. There are in fact indications that, even as resistance to product protection was growing, support for generic liberal trade policies was eroding, as some former supporters of open trade policies became less predictable, or began to favor more aggressive measures against other countries' trade practices. (We develop this more tentative conclusion, and supporting analysis, in chapter 6.)

(3) *Two primary conditions appear to determine the extent of anti-protection activity: trade dependence and threat of protection.* The greater a group's economic reliance on trade, the higher the cost it pays for protection, hence, the stronger its political opposition, other things being equal. Similarly, the

greater the threat to that trade interest, in the form of pro-protection political campaigns, the greater the activity. (Chapter 4 presents our comparative analysis of the sources of anti-protection activity.)

Several other types of influences also affect relative activity by trade-dependent interests. *Macroeconomic conditions*—inflation, the exchange rate, unemployment, and so forth—shape the political environment, especially the extent of pressures for protection, and may also affect anti-protection groups directly. Of the various *microeconomic conditions* in trade-dependent sectors, one of the most interesting is the degree to which a user of imported inputs faces *import competition for its final products*. When it does, our tentative analysis suggests, it will be more active in resisting protection for those inputs.

The *degree and form of industry political organization* can also affect behavior, even if economic conditions are the same. Actual opposition to protection is likely to be stronger the greater a group's *standing capacity for political action* on all issues. It is likely to be weaker the more that a group contains within it a *diffusion of trade interest* across many small members, *conflicting trade interests* among its members, and *competing policy priorities* other than trade.

Finally, political tactics and leadership can make a difference as well. When the pro-protection side emphasizes *charges of unfair foreign practices*, anti-protection interests are significantly less likely to speak out visibly on behalf of this trade. *Specific foreign threats of retaliation* tend to spur strong domestic anti-protection activity, although broad general threats do not appear to do so. And *leadership* by both public and private actors can stimulate a greater degree of resistance to protection than would otherwise be forthcoming.

(4) *Anti-protection activity matters.* Our final general argument is that, perhaps contrary to appearances, the growing anti-protection phenomenon has made a significant and positive difference in product cases. Political opposition in itself may not have been the most important influence on government action. Nevertheless, it did make the political process into something different from the more familiar one. In episodes in which the opposing forces mobilized greater activity, relative to their size, the trade decision tended toward rejection of protection or lesser increases. Given the US government's standing concern with alliance solidarity, and its leaders' ideological objection to protection and broader aversion to intervening in markets, visible political opposition encourages those politicians and officials to resist protection proposals. Another factor that seems to help explain

government actions is the type of labor represented by the anti-protection group: farmers and industrial workers were more successful than service workers and marketers of foreign products.

Exceptions are sometimes made for products for which the President had previously made a campaign promise, but proposals that clearly contravene US international obligations have less chance of acceptance, regardless of domestic political opposition. Still other factors probably shape trade decisions in general, but do not differentiate much among these 14 episodes. (These points are discussed in chapter 5.)

Three broad caveats   We have our own policy preferences, and they have influenced, in particular, the recommendations with which this book concludes. The primary aim of this study, however, is not to defend those preferences, but rather to describe and explain heretofore unstudied interest-group activities and their effects on government policies. We hope to produce descriptions and explanations of political behavior that will seem convincing to parties on all sides, regardless of their preferences. Therefore, as we use it, the term "protection"—which we employ in place of the invidious protection*ist*—is meant to describe an increase in restrictions on imports; it is not meant to convey pejorative implications. To describe a position as "pro-protection" is not necessarily to say that the restrictions are unjustified. We think some forms of restriction are justified in some circumstances, although we also believe that many past import barriers have been inferior to alternative policy responses. Be that as it may, an "anti-protection group" will mean any group working against a particular increase in US restrictions. Each reader is free to judge each given proposal and its critics.

The use of these terms is also not meant to suggest a mechanical, white hats-black hats view of trade politics. We agree with the common observation that the policy choices facing the United States and other governments can no longer be captured by a simple, liberal trade-protectionist dichotomy. And yet on most import issues, the dichotomy is in fact a reasonable approximation of reality; lines typically are drawn between those who want more restriction and those who want less.

That being said, the term "pro-protection" in a particular case does not mean that a group so classified was opposed to all imports of the product in question, but only that it did advocate some increase in restrictions. Nor do we assume that a group that is pro- or anti-protection in one episode is on the same "side" in all trade cases. Few anti-protection groups are pure free traders. The American Farm Bureau Federation, to cite one example, has a long history of working for trade liberalization, but has also endorsed protection against imports of some farm commodities. Wheat growers have screamed about imports; soybean producers have fought development of oilseed industries overseas. Indeed, the basic premise of this study is that important anti-protection actors are *special* interests, that their policy stands reflect importantly the impact of policy on their pocketbook. As one official interviewed for this study put it, with some exaggeration, "None of this is religion. It is economics."

Actions that restrict trade in the short run can serve the interests of open trade in the longer run. Measures that reduce imports by enforcing established trade laws can be defended as offsetting (and hence discouraging) trade distortions created by foreign firms or governments. "Protectionist" steps may also, in certain cases, broaden or preserve longer run domestic political support for open trade. Such arguments can be debated; we do not mean to deny them by use of these terms. We refer only to behavior in the context of the short-run episode under discussion.

Second, this study does not gather information in much detail on the political activity of the pro-protection side. Previous studies have already mapped that side fairly well, and to study both sides equally carefully here would not permit as deep a probe of that which is less well known. When forced to choose, we have favored depth over breadth, given the present state of knowledge. As always, this imposes a limitation, since the two sides and the government are in fact interacting. In attempting to ascertain what conditions will increase or diminish anti-protection activity, or in evaluating what determines the policy decision in a given case, the main evidence presented here provides only a partial view of the situation. We attempt to address this limitation in the chapters that follow by calling attention to considerations outside the arena studied in detail here.[1]

Our third general caveat is that private interest-group activity is not the sole or prime determinant of US trade policy. The initial stage of our analysis makes the simplifying assumption that such group struggle is relevant, and

---

1. Also for practical reasons, we have not been able systematically to investigate groups' efforts to oppose protection proposals outside the political arena. But companies sometimes contact other firms and industry associations, attempting to stop such proposals before they even reach the government, or to water them down. Such efforts have sometimes made a significant difference, as discussed later.

that other aspects can be held to one side temporarily. Later, we relax this assumption, and argue that the broader institutional, political, and economic contexts help explain how anti-protection effort has its effects.

Neither branch of the US government is a *tabula rasa* on trade, a neutral register measuring the weight of pressures; each is composed of political practitioners with their own interests and policy preferences.

Partisan politics, while generally less important than interest-group politics, is a factor also. Party interest affected recent presidential decisions on autos, textiles, and steel. And on the other side of the aisle, Democrats have intermittently seen trade as a major national issue opportunity, as do several of their presidential aspirants today.

Having made such qualifications, we move on to develop this chapter's arguments in keeping with our specific purposes. As a prelude, the next chapter introduces and summarizes each of the 14 policy episodes on which most of the analysis is based.

2 Threats of New Trade Restrictions: 14 Product Episodes

This study draws most of its empirical evidence from 14 product-specific trade cases, instances since 1974 in which a significant political effort was undertaken to increase the level of protection for specific products and industries. This set has been selected in order to contrast instances of light and heavy anti-protection effort, and to represent both relative successes and failures by such groups.

These cases form the foundation for our analysis of activity in product-specific cases in chapters 3 through 5. By no means do all US trade policy issues arise from such product-specific episodes, however. Many broad-based private groups, like the Emergency Committee for American Trade (ECAT) and the Business Roundtable, weigh in more when the issue is general legislation: what should be defined as an unfair foreign trade practice, for example. Chapter 6 examines activity in *generic* trade debates over the past fifteen years. For reasons discussed there, we did not attempt to build a comparable data base for that analysis.

The 14 episodes present neither a technically representative sample, nor a universe of possible cases, although they do include most of the product-specific proposals that would have affected large amounts of US imports during that period. Our case selection neglects, for example, those products on which there has been, over the past 14 years, no major import-restrictive initiative leading to a political decision, such as telecommunications, as well as episodes where the emphasis was at least equally on markets outside the United States, such as semiconductors. Hence, it turns out to be biased toward traditional products—sugar, steel, copper, autos, footwear, and textiles and apparel—and away from high-tech ones.

It also omits cases that did not reach the point of major *political* action in either the executive or the legislative branch: escape clause petitions rejected by the US International Trade Commission (USITC); unfair trade cases resolved within the Department of Commerce; bills that failed to reach the floor of either house of Congress. Our focus is on those episodes that went

9

far enough politically to allow competing political forces to come into play. If this selection of cases introduces any bias into the conclusions, the bias is probably against an argument that anti-protection activity matters.[1]

This chapter briefly summarizes the 14 episodes.

Sugar 1974

The Sugar Act of 1948 was due to expire on December 31, 1974. Under this statute, the Secretary of Agriculture annually assigned quotas to domestic producers and foreign countries, based on market shares as determined by Congress. In 1974, world sugar prices skyrocketed. The Secretary of Agriculture was openly hostile to renewal of the program, even though the President came out for extension. The sugar industry also had greater difficulty than previously in reaching a common position, with the growers seeking a longer extension than the refiners wanted.

Sugar-using companies and consumer organizations lobbied against extension. The House Agriculture Committee approved the bill, which included a reduction in subsidy payments to growers and repeal of the sugar excise tax. To the surprise of participants, however, the bill went down to defeat (175–209) on the House floor on June 5, 1974. Thus, the act lapsed at the end of the year, and country quotas on imports were abolished.[2]

---

1. For instance, we omit some escape clause cases in which the pro-protection side was relatively small. And we omit antidumping, countervailing duty, and escape clause cases in which the decision never reached the political level. In these administrative processes, sheer "mobilized political clout" is more difficult to bring to bear. Relative to such power, other forms of influence can have greater effects: collecting and presenting evidence to answer questions the law asks; citing precedents and offering legal interpretations to influence how officials apply the law. If mobilized clout tends to be larger on the pro-protection than on the anti-protection side, then including such cases would, if anything, probably make the evidence more favorable to the view that anti-protection activity influences decisions.

2. A nonbinding quota of 7 million tons was declared by President Ford on January 1, 1975, in order to avoid a "snapback" of the import duty to its statutory rate, as required in the Tariff Schedules of the United States (TSUS) when quotas are not in place. Headnote 2 was incorporated in the tariff schedules in the 1950s to give the President authority to modify sugar duties when quota legislation was not in effect. It sets maximum and minimum duty levels and requires that any modification of the statutory rate be accompanied by the imposition of quotas.

Footwear 1976–77

In April 1976, President Gerald R. Ford rejected a USITC recommendation of import relief for US shoe manufacturers, notwithstanding a 1974 promise by his Special Trade Representative that such a petition would receive sympathetic consideration. Instead, he ordered the secretaries of Labor and Commerce to expedite petitions for adjustment assistance received from labor or firms in the footwear industry. In September, the Senate Finance Committee asked the Commission to reopen the case.

Shortly after Jimmy Carter's inauguration, the USITC again unanimously found injury and recommended protection (in the form of tariff quotas). The new President rejected the specific recommendation but ordered negotiation of orderly marketing agreements with two major foreign suppliers, Taiwan and South Korea. These agreements went into effect in June 1977 and lasted for four years. They expired as scheduled in 1981 after President Ronald Reagan rejected a USITC recommendation that the Taiwan agreement be extended for two years. Despite the fact that only two suppliers were covered, the restraints still constituted a substantial increase in protection while they were in force.[3]

Steel 1977–78

Faced with rising imports, the US steel industry mounted a strong campaign for trade relief in 1977. The American Iron and Steel Institute kicked off the effort when it filed a section 301 petition with the Special Trade Representative late in 1976 charging that a recently concluded European-Japanese agreement on steel trade was resulting in the diversion of exports to the US market. Numerous individual dumping complaints were filed with the Department of Treasury over the next year. In addition, the industry pressed for quantitative restraints, either import quotas or negotiated export restraints. "Steel caucuses" were formed in both houses of Congress and various committees held hearings on the health of the US steel industry and enforcement of the unfair trade statutes.

The Europeans and Japanese offered to restrain their exports if the unfair

---

3. We reach this judgment by comparing the import share in the US domestic market before and after restraints. See chapter 5 and appendix D for a full explanation.

trade charges were dropped, but the Carter administration opposed quantitative limits of any kind. In October, the President endorsed an alternative: strict enforcement of the antidumping laws against what the industry argued was predatory foreign competition. A steel firm had already won a favorable preliminary ruling on a dumping petition involving Japan. Now more that twenty additional cases were initiated, with major European producers a prime target.

As the industry was pressing forward, however, the Carter administration had second thoughts. It lacked the staff to process so many unfair trade petitions expeditiously. Officials saw the likely results as trade-disruptive and inflationary. Most important, perhaps, the antidumping approach continued to be anathema to foreign governments, and it quickly became clear that the most significant findings would occur vis-à-vis European producers, threatening a crisis in US-European relations.

An interagency task force headed by Under Secretary of the Treasury Anthony Solomon devised a rather ingenious solution, the "trigger price mechanism" (TPM). The US government decided to determine floor prices for the major categories of steel products, based on the cost of production of the most efficient producers, the Japanese. Steel entering the United States below this cost would "trigger" the initiation of antidumping investigations by the Treasury Department. This solution proved acceptable to the US industry and foreign governments, and the Japanese cooperated by supplying cost-of-production data. It brought substantial new protection to the industry, but had the advantage—important to Carter economic advisers—of acting as a constraint on the pricing of domestic steel products.

Sugar 1978–79

Less than three years after their quotas had expired, sugar growers succeeded in getting Congress to approve the establishment of a mandatory price-support program. To keep imports from undermining the target price, President Carter then raised the duty on sugar to the legal maximum under authority of headnote 2 of the Tariff Schedules of the United States (TSUS). But the sugar amendment to the farm bill was effective for only two years.[4] Thus,

---

4. Because the political pattern is similar to the 1981 case, we do not include events in 1977 as a separate episode in order to avoid excessive representation for this product.

in 1978, growers proposed a new sugar act similar to the legislation that had lapsed in 1974. President Carter did not support the effort and promised to veto any program with a support price higher than 15 cents a pound. Although each house passed a sugar bill, the conference report was defeated in the House of Representatives. Producers of sweeteners were split at that point, and anti-protection groups had mounted significant political opposition, during a period of relatively rapid inflation.

In 1979 President Carter changed his position and supported sugar legislation, but with a support price lower than that desired by the growers and with reliance on fees rather than quotas to control imports. Once again the House of Representatives defeated the measure, this time by a much wider margin. The anti-protection coalition was larger and much more active than in 1978, and organized labor opposed the measure because of the wage provisions. Thus, statutorily mandated import quotas were avoided.

Autos 1980–81

The doubling of gasoline prices in the wake of the "second oil shock" of 1979 caused American consumers to cut their purchases of new cars and shift their demand toward subcompacts, a market where Japanese imports were prominent. US auto companies suddenly reported record losses and unemployment in the industry exceeded 300,000. In response, in June 1980, the United Auto Workers, later joined by Ford, submitted an escape clause petition seeking temporary import relief. In November, the US International Trade Commission announced its finding of serious injury, but (by a 3–2 vote) declared the industry ineligible for relief because dampened demand due to the recession was determined to be a more important cause of injury than imports.

Even before the USITC ruling, presidential candidate Ronald Reagan had pledged on the campaign trail to "try to convince the Japanese that . . . the deluge of their cars into the United States must be slowed." As Reagan came into office, John C. Danforth (R-Mo.), new Chairman of the Senate Finance Subcommittee on Trade, began pushing an auto quota bill in order to put pressure on the administration and the Japanese. Reagan's advisers were divided but, with strong encouragement from the White House and US Trade Representative, Japan's Ministry of International Trade and Industry announced, on May 1, 1981, that Japanese automakers would limit their

sales to the United States for the next two or three years. The April 1981–
March 1982 quota was 1.68 million units, a decline of 7.7 percent.

The restraints have been maintained until the present, even though the
Reagan administration decided in March 1985 not to request a further
extension. Fearful of the potential congressional response, the Japanese
unilaterally continued to limit shipments, though at a much higher level.
Overall, this export restraint resulted in a substantial increase in protection.

Sugar 1981–82

Though initially opposed to inclusion of sugar price supports in the 1981
farm bill, the Reagan administration withdrew its opposition to the proposed
sugar program in return for Louisiana representatives' support of its omnibus
budget-cutting resolution. Users and consumers opposed sugar supports.
Their effort to stop them on the Senate floor was rejected, but the House of
Representatives voted the bill down (190–213). House and Senate conferees
nonetheless agreed on a farm bill including the sugar program, which
Congress approved on December 12, 1981.

The legislation required the Secretary of Agriculture to support the sugar
price through loans and purchases of surplus sugar when the price falls below
the target level. The Senate Committee on Agriculture, Nutrition, and Forestry
report accompanying the farm bill urged the President "to make timely use
of his authorities under both section 22 of the Agricultural Act of 1933 and
the TSUS headnote to avoid the adverse budgetary consequences" of having
to buy up surplus sugar in case of declining prices.[5] The President embraced
the committee's suggestion of using off-budget means to support sugar prices.
In December 1981, he raised the sugar duty and imposed import fees using
section 22 authority in order to avoid having to buy and store large quantities
of sugar as the world price dropped. On May 2, 1982, with prices continuing
to fall, the Department of Agriculture, using the more flexible TSUS headnote
authority, imposed binding country-specific import quotas for the first time
since 1974.[6] The quotas slashed imports, bringing a sharp increase in new
protection to the domestic sugar industry.

---

5. In addition to the headnote authority, the President also has authority under section 22 of the
Agricultural Act of 1933 (1935 amendment) to impose quotas or fees, though not both
simultaneously, any time imports threaten to undermine an agricultural price support program.
6. The United States was required to establish country-by-country quotas as one of its obligations

Steel 1982

US steel makers brought an effective end to the trigger price mechanism on January 11, 1982, when they delivered 494 boxes containing three million pages of documentation for 132 new countervailing duty and antidumping petitions, mainly against European suppliers. The US industry had long regarded the TPM as too flexible, especially vis-à-vis Europe; Japanese steel firms had been informally restraining their exports for several years, but the flow of products across the Atlantic rose rapidly in 1981. The Reagan administration suspended enforcement of the TPM (as Carter's had temporarily, under somewhat analagous circumstances, in 1980), but it was caught in a bind, wanting neither a disruption in European relations nor new steel trade restraints. With continuing pressures at home and strong European preference for a market-sharing arrangement, Secretary of Commerce Malcolm Baldrige negotiated an agreement under which the European Community (EC) would limit carbon steel exports to roughly 5.5 percent of the US market, a substantial increase in protection for the steel industry.

Autos 1982–83

Export restraints notwithstanding, Japan's *share* of the US auto market continued to increase during the 1981–82 recession. The United Auto Workers (UAW) proposed an even more stringent remedy, legislation requiring that cars sold in the American market be governed by a rigid "domestic content" formula: the larger a company's sales volume, the greater the portion of their total value that would have to be produced in the United States, up to a maximum of 90 percent for companies like General Motors, Ford, Toyota, and Nissan. If they did not meet the formula, US sales of their cars would be drastically curtailed.

US Trade Representative (USTR) William E. Brock called it "the worst piece of economic legislation since the 1930s"; the UAW responded that it was simply a further development of the principle that the Japanese ought to put more production facilities "where their market was." With overall US unemployment at its highest level since the 1930s, the UAW called on the

---

under the International Sugar Agreement signed in 1977, but until 1982 did so at nonrestrictive levels.

loyalties of labor Democrats and won House passage by 215–188 in December 1982. Congress adjourned, however, before the legislation reached the Senate floor. In November 1983, the House voted 219–199 in favor of similar legislation, but again, the Senate took no action. By then, anti-protection interests had put together a broad coalition including car dealers, agricultural export interests, and selected consumer representatives. In addition, the US economic recovery was gathering steam, while Japan export limitations continued. By 1984, the bill was effectively dead.

Textiles 1983

In January 1983, the United States and the People's Republic of China reached an impasse in negotiations on renewal of their bilateral export restraint agreement on textiles and apparel. The Reagan administration imposed quotas unilaterally and China retaliated against US agricultural products, renouncing further purchases of cotton, soybeans, and synthetic fibers, and sharply reducing imports of corn, and most importantly, wheat. As the dispute extended into the summer, farm interests pressed the administration to soften its position, and brought in Senate Finance Committee Chairman Robert J. Dole (R-Kan.) to counter textile advocates Jesse Helms (R-NC) and Strom Thurmond (R-SC). An agreement was reached in July, and China resumed purchases of US farm products, though in reduced magnitudes. Though denounced as a "disaster" by textiles interests, the agreement contained tighter limits on export growth than the one it replaced and therefore constituted a slight increase in protection.

Textiles 1984

The textile industry acted quickly on its frustration with the US-China agreement and initiated in September 1983 a countervailing duty petition alleging that the Beijing government subsidized textile exports through the use of dual exchange rates. Partly in response, President Reagan, overruling a majority of his Cabinet, decided in December 1983 to tighten enforcement of the existing quota system against low-cost suppliers generally. The textile industry then withdrew its suit.

Against this background, in the summer of 1984 the Department of

Commerce announced changes in the rules used to attribute an imported textile or apparel item to a particular "country of origin." The stated purpose was tougher action against foreign efforts to circumvent quotas. A principal practical effect would be to curb imports of certain items of clothing from China and Hong Kong. These governments, and American retailers, reacted vociferously, claiming that sudden enforcement of these rules with only one month's notice would violate bilateral agreements, and would make them unable to fill longstanding orders. It would thus wreak havoc with the Christmas trade. They succeeded in winning first a postponement of their enforcement, then a slight modification of their content. Tightened regulations finally went into effect in April 1985, thus providing a slight increase in protection for the textile and apparel industries.[7]

Copper 1984

US copper mines, suffering from import competition and depressed world prices, petitioned the US International Trade Commission for trade relief in January 1984. The USITC found injury in July and recommended trade relief: two commissioners proposed a tariff of 5 cents a pound, and two others recommended quotas. The President was required to act within 60 days, in the midst of his campaign for reelection.

Users of copper, primarily fabricators, saw import restrictions as a threat to them: protection for their input would raise their production costs and increase their vulnerability to foreign competition. The fabricators launched a strong anti-protection campaign, arguing that quotas or tariffs would induce a sharp increase in imports of copper products, hurting them and depriving the petitioners of much of their gain. They noted further that they employed several times as many workers as the mines, so that the electoral advantages lay on their side of the issue.

Copper mine representatives recognized that protection would be of limited benefit to them and devastate their customers. So they proposed to the White House what they had wanted all along: negotiation of a global *production* limitation agreement that would raise prices worldwide, helping US producers

---

7. For a comprehensive economic analysis of textile protection in the United States, see William R. Cline, *The Future of World Trade in Textiles and Apparel* (Washington: Institute for International Economics, September 1987).

without disadvantaging the fabricators. But the representatives of exporting nations disputed US industry contentions that they too would be net gainers from such an arrangement, and free-market-oriented Reagan administration economic officials reacted sharply against an "OPEC for copper." The fabricators, initially receptive to the production restraint proposal, settled on a simple stance of opposing import relief. They won when Reagan determined in early September that import restraints were "not in the international economic interest of the United States."

Producers succeeded in attaching to trade legislation passed in 1984 a weak, sense-of-Congress resolution requiring the President either to negotiate international production restraints or to explain to Congress why he had not. But as generally anticipated, he did the latter. So the mines' campaign ended in failure.

Steel 1984

Even with restraints on exports from the European Community and Japan, carbon steel imports continued to rise after 1982, predominantly from countries not covered by existing restraints, such as Korea, Brazil, and Mexico. The industry responded in early 1984 with a three-pronged campaign: support of a statutory quota bill; initiation of new countervailing duty and antidumping suits; and an escape clause petition. It was the latter that forced presidential action. The USITC found injury and recommended relief in the form of tariffs and quotas covering 70 percent of steel imports for five years.

President Reagan, in the September of his reelection campaign, formally rejected the Commission recommendation in the name of free trade, but had USTR Brock announce at the same time the administration's intention of negotiating export restraint agreements with all other major foreign suppliers, to be effective until 1989. The aim was to bring imports down to the "more normal level" of "approximately 18 percent" of the US market, "excluding semifinished steel." Congress quickly added a steel program enforcement title to the pending Trade and Tariff Act of 1984. Since the new system was to cover all major foreign sources, it represented substantial new protection for the domestic industry.

Footwear 1984–85

The US footwear industry sought escape clause relief again in January 1984, timing its petition—reportedly—to put pressure on the President during his reelection campaign. The USITC, however, found profits high, despite rising imports, and, hence, no "serious injury." One factor in the case was the active information campaign by the footwear retailers, who stressed the central role that imports were playing, not just in retail markets, but in the operations of the producers themselves.

Industry advocate Senator John Danforth signaled his displeasure with the decision by winning modification of the escape clause statute, specifying that "the presence or absence of any factor [for example, profits] which the Commission is required to evaluate" should not be "dispositive." This signal was reinforced when the Finance Committee exercised its prerogative of asking the USITC to reopen the case. Meanwhile, imports had increased further and industry profits had turned downward. The USITC now found injury and, in summer 1985, recommended relief in the form of auctioned quotas. Again the Footwear Retailers of America were active in countering the producers' campaign. In August, President Reagan decided against import relief on broad anti-protection grounds.

Textiles 1985–86

Early in 1985, Representative Ed Jenkins (D-Ga.) introduced a textile industry bill that would have substantially cut textile and apparel imports, which had surged enormously in 1984. At first, neither the industry nor its adversaries seem to have viewed it as serious legislation. Benefiting from administration neglect and an explosion of congressional trade concerns in the wake of a $100 billion-plus trade deficit, however, the bill took off, with a majority of senators and over 290 representatives signing on as co-sponsors.

Retailers became a focal point of opposition to the bill. The Retail Industry Trade Action Coalition (RITAC) conducted a broad anti-protection campaign in member department stores and congressional offices. The Reagan administration got better organized. The American Textile Manufacturers Institute pressed ahead, but procedural maneuvering blocked their effort to get the proposal to the Senate floor that summer. By the time it came to a House vote on October 10, its adversaries had been able to target and "peel off" about 30 co-sponsors, and the House vote of 262–159 was well short of what was necessary to override a presidential veto.

The Senate moderated the textile provisions somewhat, reducing the number of countries targeted for rollback from 12 to 3 (thus excluding China and Brazil), but added provisions attacking shoe and copper imports. It passed the legislation by a comparable margin, 60–39. The House accepted the Senate version and sent the bill on to President Reagan, who vetoed it in December.

The textile industry's congressional advocates then staged a procedural coup. Normally, efforts to overturn presidential vetoes take place shortly thereafter, or they do not take place at all. But Jenkins bill proponents were able to get the vote on overriding this veto scheduled for eight months later, the following August, just after the scheduled completion of negotiations on renewal of the Multi-Fiber Arrangement (MFA). This enabled the textile and apparel producers to keep the pressure on administration negotiators, to achieve by negotiation at least part of what they wanted.

With the forthcoming summer vote hanging over their heads, executive officials responded to some extent. In bilateral talks, the US Trade Representative persuaded the leading foreign suppliers—Hong Kong, Taiwan, and South Korea—to accept new agreements cutting their growth rates to less than 1 percent per year. In the MFA talks, the administration took a harder line than the EC, refusing to accept liberalization of these long-standing restrictions, and insisting on broadening them to permit limits on fibers never before controlled. Even so, US producers denounced these pacts for being too loose and not actually cutting imports. In an atmosphere dominated by the enormous overall US trade deficit, and after heavy lobbying on all sides, including by Reagan himself, the bill won substantially more House votes than it had the previous September. Still, the industry fell eight votes short of the two-thirds majority needed to override the veto. It is too early to judge the full impact of the stricter MFA provisions, but just the new bilaterals with the top three suppliers constitute at least slight new protection for the US industry.

Summary

These cases represent a mix of products and outcomes. Five of them resulted in victories for anti-protection interests: no import barriers, or removal of existing ones. The President rejected escape clause relief for copper in 1984 and footwear in 1985; the domestic content bill (autos 1982–83) passed its prime; sugar quotas lapsed in 1974 along with the broader legislation. Sugar campaigns in 1978 and 1979 to reenact a program for that commodity were also defeated.

In one other case, sugar 1981–82 the outcome was the opposite: a sharp increase in protection. Five others resulted in more limited but still substantial new protection: restrictive agreements with one or a few suppliers (autos 1980–81, footwear 1977, steel 1982), and the TPM for steel 1977–78. The three textile cases resulted in slight increases in protection as a result of tighter enforcement of existing restrictions.

Of course, treating each of these episodes as purely independent would be to ignore clear threads of historical continuity from one year to the next in sectors like sugar and textiles. On the other hand, to treat various episodes concerning a product like sugar as a single case would obscure striking oscillations in political activity and in policy direction from one episode to another. We thus define cases so as to try to achieve the greatest possible analytical yield, and we also bring out the points at which one episode is influencd by others.

Having described the trade episodes that serve as our study's primary base, we move now to the three central questions of this study: what anti-protection interests are active in US trade politics; why; and what has been the impact of such activity on US trade policy?

3 The Rise of Anti-Protection Political Activity: A Look at the Primary Interests

Political resistance to proposals for product-specific trade protection increased sharply between the mid-1970s and the mid-1980s. The primary groups contributing to this rise were not household consumers, and not—taken as a whole—the multinational corporations or the business-coalition organizations that carried the free trade banner in the past. Rather, the most active anti-protection groups were four types of special interests benefiting particularly from the trade threatened with restriction: industrial users of imports, retailers of traded consumer goods, US exporters selling to the countries whose products were targeted, and the companies and governments of those countries.

This chapter presents broad evidence of this increase, and examines its composition: which groups acted in the 14 episodes just described and which did not. It looks in some detail at specific categories of anti-protection groups, exploring concrete instances of their activity (and, in some instances, lack of activity). In so doing it not only presents information important in its own right, but builds a basis for the comprehensive analysis presented in chapter 4.

Defining Activity

"Activity" refers to steps taken by individuals or groups to influence government decisionmaking on a particular trade issue. This includes, but is by no means limited to, activity by professional lobbyists. We count activity as *anti-protection* when the stated preference of the actor is to prevent or minimize new trade restrictions.[1]

We differentiate among degrees or levels of activity—low, medium, high—by not only the volume but also the type of actions taken, as illustrated by the following table:

---

1. In general, differentiating *anti-protection* activity from neutrality or a stand in favor of new

TABLE 3.1 **Levels of activity**

Low	Medium	High
Joining a coalition	Testimony to Congress	Leading a coalition
Scattered official	Selective lobbying	Broad lobbying
contacts	Hiring a law firm	Big, organized campaign
Press release or two	Taking initiative regarding con-	Mobilizing of constituents
Signing a joint letter	stituents, other organizations	

At the lowest level above inaction, individual constituents send scattered communications to officials—executive, legislative, or both—or their trade association puts its name on a joint letter, along with other organizations. Some information may be prepared on how a proposed measure would affect their interests, or a press release or two may be issued.

Moderate political activity includes these steps but goes beyond them as an interest group commits more resources, or takes more risks. It may testify before a congressional committee, or take the initiative in inviting others to join in a coalition, or hire a law firm to present a formal brief before the US International Trade Commission (USITC). Such activity will include selective lobbying of officials who can influence a decision, and probably some limited efforts to raise constituents' awareness and stimulate them to contact Washington.

In cases of heavy activity, large resources are committed. The issue

---

restrictions presents no problem, but in borderline situations finer distinctions must be drawn. In one case, for example, a group testified that it opposed protection as a first preference, but also that it would prefer a negotiated export restraint to enforcement of the US antidumping law. In this and similar cases, we counted the activity as anti-protection since clear opposition to restraints was expressed, and we interpreted the qualification as a second-best choice, an attempt to have some practical effect on a situation in which total rejection of new barriers seemed unlikely. Similarly, exporters and governments of other countries are usually taken as preferring no new restrictions at all, even if, under pressure, they also offer to negotiate export restraints at some point in the episode.

We include in the anti-protection camp groups that oppose only restrictions for certain product categories among those threatened in an episode, as well as those taking broader stands. Some special interests avoid the political arena unless their specific interests are affected, and then focus their activity narrowly. On the other hand, if a firm or organization makes no clear statement opposing protection on some product, or if it testifies only in support of, say, measures against unfair imports, such activity is not counted here, even if the group appears to have a stake in continuing trade.

becomes one of the organization's top priorities in the government policy arena. Its Washington representatives are likely to play a lead role in coalitions meeting every week or two; they conduct broad, organized lobbying campaigns on Capitol Hill and downtown; they prepare extensive position papers, they work closely with congressional and executive branch friends in developing strategy, tactics, and specific proposals, and they organize heavy mail and personal visits from important constituents in home states and districts.

The Rise of Anti-Protection Activity

While anti-protection activity cannot be measured with precision, our data suggest there has been a substantial rise, perhaps even a multiplication, over the past decade. For each of the 14 product cases summarized in chapter 2, we have developed as comprehensive as possible a list of groups involved in campaigns against new trade restrictions (appendix A presents these lists). Included are individual companies working alone, and standing associations of enterprises in the same line of business acting as a unit. Ad hoc coalitions sharing a similar international trade interest, like the Sugar Users Group, have been prominent in certain episodes. "Umbrella" or "conglomerate" commercial organizations, spanning many different sectors of the economy, like the Chamber of Commerce of the United States, the American Farm Bureau Federation, or the Emergency Committee for American Trade (ECAT), appear occasionally. So do nonprofit organizations like the League of Women Voters and Consumers for World Trade. The International Longshoremen's Association is one of the few labor unions to have acted on the anti-protection side. Finally, producers and governments of foreign companies have participated, a few of them quite heavily, in recent episodes.

In order to get a rough sense of the magnitude of opposition in each episode and to ascertain trends, we apply a simple scoring procedure. We assign a rating to each group's activity in each episode, setting scores so as to reflect, at least crudely, differences in level. Light, moderate, and heavy efforts were initially assigned scores of 1, 5, and 25, respectively, with adjustments to reflect variations within each category.[2] Summing the scores for all groups acting in an episode yields an aggregate activity rating for that episode (see table 3.2).

---

2. Appendix A explains this procedure, and shows the numerical ratings for each group in each episode.

TABLE 3.2   **Aggregate activity in product episodes**

Case	Rating
Sugar 1974	19
Footwear 1976–77	129
Steel 1977–78	33
Sugar 1978–79	72
Autos 1980–81	117
Sugar 1981–82	48
Steel 1982	61
Autos 1982–83	337
Textiles 1983	52
Textiles 1984	126
Copper 1984	103
Steel 1984	335
Footwear 1984–85	182
Textiles 1985–86	280

These numbers should be viewed as very rough indicators, not precise measures. They reflect the qualitative judgments of the authors. Furthermore, they may be skewed slightly in favor of more recent episodes, since memories of those interviewed were fresher concerning them. Still, one cannot but be impressed by how much larger the ratings are in later cases than in earlier ones. The average rating for the first seven is 68; the average for the last seven is 202! Chronological comparisons for individual products also show, in almost all cases, a striking rise in anti-protection activity from episode to episode. And these antiseptic-looking numbers incorporate some dramatic examples from recent trade-political history: wheat exporters fighting textile interests concerning the China trade, copper users countering proposals for import restraint, and auto dealers mobolizing against domestic content legislation.

Explaining the Rise: Three Large Reasons

This broad, aggregate trend was the product of a range of forces operating on particular groups in diverse ways. Some influences were present in some episodes and absent in others, and our analysis in chapter 4 seeks to assess their relative importance. However, three major forces seem to have been particularly important.

AN INCREASE IN THREATS

One, of course, is the rise in pro-protection activity and the increased ambitiousness of protectionist proposals. For steel, autos, footwear, and automobiles, the most recent episode—which generated the most anti-protection activity—also featured the proposal that would most restrict trade (see chapter 2). Two other forces deserve attention here. The first is the rise in the overall trade dependence of the US economy. The second is the broader explosion of lobbying activity in Washington.

THE GROWTH OF US TRADE DEPENDENCE

Over the years, foreign trade has become very big business to a growing number of special interests that benefit from it. The US economy has changed structurally toward greater reliance on international trade. From 1960 to 1970 to 1980 the value of merchandise exports plus imports tripled in proportion to US goods production, from 14 percent to 18 percent to 42 percent, even with the much documented increase in trade protection after 1970. Some of this increase was due to volume changes and some to price changes, particularly for oil and other commodities. But on a volume (price-deflated) basis, the proportion also rose substantially, from 19 percent in 1970 to 25 percent in 1980 and 26 percent in 1985.[3]

More than half of US imports in the early 1980s went not to household consumers but to manufacturers and farmers who use imports of materials and machinery in their production processes. If restraints are imposed against imports of steel, copper, or semiconductors, users must either cut profits or raise the prices they charge for their end products, thereby undermining their competitiveness.[4] Imports of consumer goods affect the interests not only of

---

3. For a broader discussion of this distinction and the export and import data, see I. M. Destler, *American Trade Politics: System Under Stress* (Washington and New York, NY: Institute for International Economics and Twentieth Century Fund, 1986), pp. 168–72.

4. This was the reason that the United States did not impose retaliatory tariffs on Japanese semiconductors in the spring 1987 dispute, but on downstream electronics products that contained

the (typically unorganized) final buyers, but also distributors and retailers who compete by offering foreign goods.

This internationalization of the US economy has broadened the set of special interests, based within our borders, that would suffer from import restrictions. We would expect that at least some of them would become politically engaged when trade-restrictive proposals threatened their interests.

THE EXPLOSION IN ORGANIZED CAPACITY FOR POLITICAL ACTION

Trade politics has also been affected by the transformation of the Washington policy community over the last two decades. There has been "a veritable explosion in the number of groups lobbying in Washington" on all issues.[5] The standing private organizational capacity for political action expanded enormously. This institutional change probably led to greater actual interest-group activity on trade than would have occurred from economic changes alone, and it may continue to do so.

The organizational explosion was in several ways a response to broader changes in US government and politics. After the 1960s, political authority in the Congress fragmented more than before, as new members challenged the seniority system's grip on committee chairmanships. In the House of Representatives, the number of subcommittees multiplied, and the top leadership lost some of what former ability it had had to control the legislative process. Thus, any interest-group lobbyist, whether concerned about taxes, endangered species, abortion, or trade, found that he or she needed to contact far more members than before in order to monitor and have the same effect on a legislative outcome. More hands were needed on a more continuous basis.

New laws in the 1960s and 1970s also created more regulations, concerned with pollution, job safety, and other issues, and business in particular reacted to these. The arrival of more business lobbyists also interacted with the rise of a more vocal adversary, the "public interest" and consumer lobbies. More and more individual companies established their own presences in Washington. According to one study, the number of companies represented by registered

---

chips as an input. Even so, it required two days of hearings for no less than 74 organized interests to be heard about why imports on which *they* depended should not be subject to trade sanctions!

5. Allan J. Cigler and Burdett A. Loomis, eds., *Interest Group Politics*, 2d ed. (Washington: Congressional Quarterly Press, 1986), p. 9.

lobbyists in Washington jumped from 130 in 1961 to 650 in 1979, and the number maintaining their own Washington offices went from 50 to 247. Moreover, the function of these offices expanded greatly from essentially sales, to gaining access to and influencing the policy process.[6] They crowded around the offices of the industry associations already present. According to one source, the officers of trade and professional associations and labor unions permanently based in the capital numbered about 3,500 in 1985.[7] Another rough indicator of the proliferation is the tripling in the number of attorneys in the city between 1973 and 1983.[8]

Business representatives also gained increasing experience after the mid-1970s in the formation of ad hoc Washington coalitions on policy issues other than trade.[9] A single group can sometimes generate additional supporting activity by other groups with similar interests, more than would have appeared spontaneously, by taking the initiative and providing the leadership in a coalition.

The result of all this was to swell groups' standing capacity to monitor government in detail and to bring information and pressure to bear relatively quickly. The development of computerized, direct-mail technology also expanded possibilities for alerting constituents and mobilizing pressure back home as well. Some larger individual companies have developed sophisticated private networks among their "grass roots"—shareholders, retirees, and employees—which can be activated in pursuit of selected company public policy goals.[10]

---

6. David B. Yoffie and Sigrid Bergenstein, "Creating Political Advantage: The Rise of the Corporate Political Entrepreneur," *California Management Review,* vol. 28, no. 1 (Fall 1985), p. 125. See also Phyllis S. McGrath, *Redefining Corporate-Federal Relations* (New York, NY: The Conference Board, 1979).

7. Arthur Close and Jody Curtis, eds., *Washington Representatives 1985* (New York, NY: Columbia Books, Inc., 1985).

8. Cigler and Loomis, p. 10. For discussion of this trend nationwide, and its relation to other US political developments, see Nelson W. Polsby, "Contemporary Transformations of American Politics: Thoughts on the Research Agendas of Political Scientists," *Political Science Quarterly,* vol. 96, no. 4 (Winter 1981–82), esp. pp. 564–65.

9. See Sar A. Levitan and Martha R. Cooper, *Business Lobbies: The Public Good and the Bottom Line* (Baltimore, Md.: Johns Hopkins University Press, 1984); "Coalitions and Associations Transform Strategy, Methods of Lobbying in Washington," *Congressional Quarterly Weekly Report,* 23 January 1982, pp. 119–123.

10. "Companies Organize Employees and Holders into a Political Force," *Wall Street Journal,* 15 August 1978; Gerry Keim, "Corporate Grassroots Programs in the 1980s," *California Management Review,* vol. 28 (Fall 1985), pp. 110–23.

Finally, some group representatives have been becoming much better informed about international trade issues in the last few years. Before then, many business association executives had had no experience with such issues, and were not likely to screen government developments specifically to identify threats that imports or protection proposals might pose for their employers and clients. To be sure, much of the learning has been motivated by the wish to combat foreign competition better themselves. But part of that learning is a greater sensitivity to costs and efficiency. Some organizations used the techniques and contacts they had developed on other issues to build coalitions and rally constituents against import protection, as illustrated later in this chapter.

These enlarged political capabilities will not be used on future trade issues simply because they exist. But now that all these Washington representatives are in place, they will be attempting to generate work on some issue. If the organizational expansion is not reversed, then even if international market conditions should change, observed political pressure, from both pro- and anti-protection sides, may not decline as much as the economic change would imply.

Granted that there has been a rise in anti-protection activity, what groups have led the way? More generally, what specific types of interests based within the US economy benefit most from trade? The remainder of this chapter analyzes the political activity of such groups, first by asking which ones might be expected to resist proposed trade restrictions (who "ought" to act), and examining who in fact has done so and who has not.[11] Then chapter 4 presents a more comprehensive set of hypotheses concerning conditions that stimulate or diminish campaigns like these, together with relevant quantitative and qualitative evidence.

General Anti-Protection Interests

As a rule, *general trade interests* are much less active in resisting protection for specific products than *special trade interests*.

---

11. Here, as throughout the core of this study, we focus on episodes concerning trade in particular products. In these episodes, players often take US political institutions and laws as given and work within them. In chapter 6, we examine such groups' efforts to influence generic trade policy, including proposals that would have changed the law and the policy-making and administrative institutions themselves.

By general trade interests, we mean groups whose members taken together gain broadly from trade, but only marginally from trade in a given product. Within this category we would place:

- *household consumers*

- *multinational corporations*, including large money center banks, and the organizations that represent them (for example, the Emergency Committee for American Trade [ECAT])

- *business coalition organizations* with broad memberships, like the National Association of Manufacturers, the Chamber of Commerce, and the American Farm Bureau Federation.

These groups tend to be weakened, despite their large sizes, by the classic collective-goods or free-rider problem, or by diverging interests among their members.

HOUSEHOLD CONSUMERS

Costs to consumers—in higher prices for both foreign and domestic goods—are a staple of economic analyses of the costs of trade protection.[12] Yet the failure of consumers to act on this interest is a staple of political analysis. Consumers of shoes, for instance, face a severe collective action problem. Political activity costs time and money, and each individual buyer among millions has an incentive to "let George do it." And, of course, a large share of consumers are also producers of goods, and, when they think about trade politics, they may well worry more about their jobs than about paying a higher price for sandals.

Our examination of anti-protection activity confirms, for the most part, this conventional trade-political wisdom. Consumers engage in far less political activity—and take less consistently anti-protection stands—than would seem to be indicated by their trade interests. There have been some

---

12. Gary Clyde Hufbauer, Diane T. Berliner, and Kimberly Ann Elliott, in *Trade Protection in the United States: 31 Case Studies* (Washington: Institute for International Economics, 1986), apply a common methodology across a range of products and conclude that "special protection," in the form of quotas, very high tariffs, or both, costs consumers $27 billion in 1984 for textiles and apparel, $6.8 billion for steel, and $5.8 billion for automobiles. A rough estimate of the total cost to consumers of special protection in all sectors in 1986 is $65 billion.

significant exceptions, on the part of consumer organizations. Consumers Union (CU) went to court in the early 1970s to block enforcement of "voluntary" restraints on steel imports. CU has also spoken out against import barriers on cars. The Consumer Federation of America (CFA) has testified periodically in opposition to high sugar prices, although it has sometimes stressed causes other than import restraints, such as alleged large mark-ups by sugar refiners. In 1979, a coalition of major consumer organizations lobbied fairly widely against the sugar bill.[13] But the CFA actually endorsed the domestic content legislation for automobiles in 1982, though not without hot internal debate. The apparent reason was the longstanding alliance of the consumer movement with organized labor on those issues—like truth-in-packaging or product safety—to which the movement has given much higher priority than international trade.[14]

Otherwise, virtually the only consumer activity we have found has been the work of a Washington-based organization. In the 1980s, Consumers for World Trade (CWT) has resisted product-specific import restrictions fairly consistently. CWT grew from a coalition of more than twenty nonprofit membership organizations (for example, the National Council of Jewish Women) which came together to fight the Burke-Hartke quota bill of the early 1970s. CWT has now made itself a visible anti-protection lobby on the Washington scene. It has testified frequently before Congress, against auto, steel, and textile protection, and tried to lead a coalition against the 1984 steel campaign. CWT commissions or publishes estimates of how much consumers pay for restrictions like the voluntary restraint agreement (VRA) on autos. But despite its origins, the organizers have to date been unable to build a broad consumer base. Its membership is only a thousand, and its board of directors is composed mainly of people who have come to their liberal trade views for nonconsumer reasons. The mainline consumer organizations have largely kept their distance.

---

13. Based partly on an interview with a participant in the coalition. See appendix A for a discussion of research sources and methods. We follow the convention that any statement in the text based solely or predominantly on a private interview will be so identified. We do not, however, cite information that is provided in our appendices, or that is available in widely circulated periodicals like the *New York Times* or *Congressional Quarterly* (another source for the information provided above). Appendix A lists those periodicals used systematically, and it identifies each specific group known to be active in each product-specific episode.

14. CFA's Executive Director told the *Wall Street Journal* (3 September 1982): "On the surface, this might appear to go against consumer interests," but "we appreciate all the work for consumer issues that the UAW has done over the years."

MULTINATIONAL CORPORATIONS

A second set of interests with broad stakes in the open world economy is the major multinational corporations (MNCs). But a look at who has been active in our 14 product episodes finds them, on balance, no more visible than consumer groups. One multinational corporation, Caterpillar, Inc., does appear on the heavy activity list for one episode, steel 1984, but this can be explained—as discussed later in this chapter—by its status as a major steel user. In general, MNCs have not been significant, visible political players in these struggles, although it is certainly possible that their officers have communicated with government officials through private channels.[15] Nor are organizations representing them—ECAT, the Business Roundtable—prominent in our episode-specific activity lists (although they have been considerably more important players on generic trade issues, as discussed in chapter 6).

At least three constraints limit MNC activity in this sort of case. First, a new restriction on copper or textiles in and of itself will often cost a firm like IBM, Pfizer, or Citibank too little to convince them to undertake the expense and risk of political activity. Second, a given multinational firm or bank is often home to conflicting interests. One division might suffer from a proposed steel barrier, while another division produces in competition with the imports to be restricted. The international loan officers of a large bank probably would prefer to see the bank do battle against restrictions that would hurt "their" countries, but often another division will be working hard to cultivate the US industry (or the US politicians) campaigning for the restrictions. Banks have typically been cross-pressured into silence on trade issues. By extension, organizations combining multinationals from different industries include both winners and losers from the typical product-specific proposal; hence, their leaders find their efforts to oppose the measure blocked within the organization.

Third, multinational firms are global investors. As such they have specific

---

15. Other research indicates that exporters and governments in other countries have managed on occasion to activate such communications on their behalf from US companies having a stake in those countries. While the known steps helped dilute the campaign for protection, they did not make dramatic differences in decisions. (John S. Odell, "Latin American Trade Negotiations with the United States," *International Organization,* vol. 34 (Spring 1980), pp. 207–28.) This study's interviews turned up only scattered evidence of behind-the-scenes pressure. The trend, however, is probably toward more and more sophisticated foreign tactical use of direct contacts with US overseas investors in economic disputes.

alternatives to politics, and they have political priorities other than trade. The defining characteristic of such a firm is that it owns a global network of operations rooted in many countries, with each unit often designed to sell in its respective domestic market as much as to trade internationally.[16] Although all multinationals would be upset by a large-scale disruption of the world trade system, short of that, their global networks offer them alternative, commercial strategies for adjusting to trade barriers, such as shifting sources of production from one country to another. This commercial option reduces their need to enter political arenas.

And when they do, other goals may take priority. A multinational company does not necessarily earn a large share of its revenue directly from US exports or US imports. For example, in 1983 exports from the US were only 9 percent of General Motors sales; figures for other global firms were: ITT, 5 percent; E. I. du Pont, 7 percent; IBM, 6 percent; General Electric, 16 percent; and Dow Chemical, 8 percent.[17] The interest such multinationals have most in common is the treatment of foreign investment and its income by US and other governments' regulations and tax laws. So when they operate as a group in Washington, they tend to give priority to such issues, with trade getting, at best, secondary priority.

BUSINESS COALITION ORGANIZATIONS

The same internal conflicts that can beset MNCs on product issues also affect multi-sector business organizations like the National Association of Manufacturers or the Chamber of Commerce. Not surprisingly, we find that they too are sparsely represented in the population of active groups on product issues. The Chamber was a heavy actor, however, in the one product-specific trade campaign with the broadest potential impact on general US trade policy, the drive for domestic content requirements for automobile production. Such organizations generally have been more active on generic trade issues (chapter 6).

---

16. For elaboration, see C. Fred Bergsten, Thomas Horst, and Theodore H. Moran, *American Multinationals and American Interests* (Washington: Brookings Institution, 1978).

17. *Fortune*, 6 August 1984, p. 65.

Special Anti-Protection Interests

Special trade interests are much more directly affected by specific product import restrictions, and they have been much more active. Within this category the main types of groups are:

- *exporters*, those who produce for foreign markets

- *business and industrial import users*, those for whom imported products are an important production input

- *retailers and other trade-related services*, such as importers and port and transportation interests

- *governments and producers of exporting countries*.

EXPORTERS

Who are the export interests? We get a beginning answer from broad trade statistics. Table 3.3 shows the US products whose net exports were greatest in 1981, when US international accounts were in balance, and in 1985, when the nation ran a very large trade deficit. We get a familiar list dominated in 1985 by agriculture and high-technology manufacturing: cereals rank at the top, followed by chemicals, aircraft, soybeans, coal, office machinery, and scientific instruments. We also see the sharp drop in net exports most of these producers suffered as the high dollar undercut their competitive position. The impact was particularly acute for most types of industrial machinery, whose trade—and rank on the list—fell off sharply.

This list shows gross export dependence. But those with the largest volume were not necessarily the sectors most dependent on exports relative to total sales. Many of these producers—such as those in chemicals, office machinery, and coal—sell heavily in the US market as well. Their political involvement in trade may be a product of their absolute level of trade. But they may also weigh the importance of trade, and hence the cost of protection, relative to their total business, in deciding whether acting politically is worthwhile.

To get at this relative dependence, table 3.4 ranks larger exporters according to the degree of their dependence on exports. This ranking elevates a number of smaller sectors above some larger ones in the former table. In 1981, the most dependent were wheat, with an export-production ratio of .77, tractors at .63, cotton at .52, soybeans at .50, and aircraft at .45, with many smaller

TABLE 3.3   **Leading net exporters by product group, 1981 and 1985**
(million dollars)

Rank			Net exports	
1981	*1985*	*Product*	*1981*	*1985*
1	1	Cereals and cereal products	19,181	15,547
2	2	Chemicals and related products	13,244	8,639
3	3	Aircraft and parts	12,050	7,903
4	8	Specialized industrial machinery	9,949	2,560
5	4	Soybeans	6,200	5,350
6	6	Office machinery	6,090	3,801
7	13	General industrial machinery	5,970	1,019
8	5	Coal, coke, and briquets	5,863	4,219
9	12	Power generating machinery and equipment	4,869	1,823
10	7	Professional, scientific, and controlling instruments	4,213	3,502
11	10	Animal feed (not including unmilled cereals)	2,602	2,141
12	9	Raw cotton	2,260	2,417
13	11	Tobacco and tobacco manufactures	1,972	2,006

Source: OECD, Trade Series C, and US Department of Commerce, *Highlights of US Export and Import Trade,* FT 990, various issues.

categories of manufactured products (for example, instruments to measure electricity) having numbers over .30. Table 3.4 reveals significant differences in aggregate export stakes, for example contrasting wheat and corn, and it also uncovers some less visible sectors that seem to have quite strong interests in exports.[18]

Such numbers suggest strong trade stakes. If active, producers of these products would form a formidable coalition in support of open trade policies. And in fact, many of the export interests represented in tables 3.3 and 3.4 have been consistently available, "on call" to support negotiations aimed at trade expansion through reciprocal reduction of import barriers. One important reason, of course, is that they stand to gain directly from easing of foreign import barriers.

---

18. Numbers are included for total value of production as an indicator of industry size.

TABLE 3.4   **The ratio of exports to production, and value of production for selected products, 1981 and 1985**

Product	Exports/ production (percentage)		Production (million dollars)	
	1981	1985	1981	1985
Wheat	77	47	10,196	7,652
Tractors and parts	63	49	5,700	3,754
Cotton	52	47	4,337	3,507
Soybeans	50	36	12,281	10,757
Aircraft, spacecraft, and parts	45	31	32,176	46,030
Mechanical shovels, excavators, etc.	42	23	17,400	19,735
Semiconductors	42	34	8,671	12,500
Instruments for physical and chemical analysis	40	25	2,270	3,450
Corn	39	19	20,502	28,327
Rice	32	9	1,687	1,075
Fertilizer and materials	31	29	8,900	9,206
Motor vehicle parts	30	30	23,120	30,604
Instruments for measuring electricity	31	24	4,300	6,800
Steam generating boilers	28	13	2,357	2,892
Manmade filament yarn	25	20	2,632	2,139

Source: US International Trade Commission, *US Trade Shifts in Selected Commodity Areas,* Annual Reports 1982 and 1986, Washington.

But do these producers have similar stakes in resisting specific proposals to restrict imports? At the broadest level, of course, US import restrictions reduce the income of America's foreign customers taken as a whole, and thus reduce total US products foreigners can buy. But this leaves open the question of whose exports will be affected how much. What specific export interests can expect to bear a disproportionate burden, to pay particular costs as a result of particular trade restrictions?

One likely answer would be those with important markets in the particular foreign countries whose products were the target of trade-restrictive proposals.

TABLE 3.5   **Key US export sectors in 1983 textiles case: major 1982 exports to China**

SITC	SIC	Commodity
0410	0111	Wheat
2631	0131	Cotton
6114	3111	Leather
2471	2411	Softwood logs[a]
6514	2281	Yarn of nylon, polyester, etc.[b]
5629	2873	Fertilizers n.s.p.f.[c]
5881	2821	Synthetic resins n.e.c.
2665	2824	Noncellulosic fibers n.s.p.f. (manmade)
0440	0115	Corn
2222	0116	Soybeans

SITC   Standard International Trade Classification; SIC   Standard Industrial Classification; n.s.p.f.   not specifically provided for; n.e.c.   not elsewhere classified.
Source: US Department of Commerce, *US Exports,* FT 455, *U.S. Industrial Outlook,* and *Statistical Abstract of the United States,* various years; and US Department of Agriculture, *Agricultural Statistics,* various years.

Such exporters would pay costs, in the sense that those countries' general capacity to buy abroad is reduced by curbs on their exports. But they might also fear more direct costs in the form of retaliation.

To evaluate exporters' anti-protection interests, it is helpful to get down to cases. To this end, we have examined US trade data to determine which sectors of the US economy were most dependent on sales to the principal foreign countries that were targets of particular product protection campaigns. The tables in appendix B rank export interests in each case according to their degree of dependence on exports to the targeted countries.[19] Each table

---

19. We omit the sugar cases, because major exporting nations in fact *supported* the country-based quota system in 1974, and were not active in opposing proposed quotas in 1978–79. Thus US exporters had no reason to fear retaliation against their sales.

Target's share of shipments	Ratio of exports to shipments	Target's share of exports	Exports to target	Total exports	Total shipments
	(percentage)			(million dollars)	
0.107	0.680	0.157	1,047	6,676	9,813
0.052	0.573	0.091	178	1,955	3,410
0.044	0.141	0.313	65	208	1,474
0.032	0.176	0.181	212	1,174	6,668
0.025	0.112	0.228	115	504	4,520
0.025	0.230	0.110	86	782	3,399
0.013	0.137	0.098	236	2,420	17,615
0.013	0.039	0.327	91	278	7,150
0.009	0.258	0.033	189	5,683	22,039
0.005	0.501	0.010	63	6,240	12,463

a. Total exports and shipments include hardwood logs, which have averaged less than 10 percent of exports and less than 20 percent of shipments in recent years.
b. Shipments include cotton yarn.
c. Imports of fertilizers under SITC 5629 are other than phosphatic; shipments under SIC 2873 are of nitrogenous fertilizers.

examines exports for the year prior to that of the primary protection threat, on the grounds that that year's experience will be most relevant to affected interests while the issue is being fought out. For example, table 3.5 shows principal US exports to the People's Republic of China in 1982, the year prior to US tightening of textile import restrictions on that country's products.

In general, the product interests ranking high in the appendix B tables correspond to those export-dependent groups highlighted earlier. Wheat, soybean, and corn farmers were among the six most dependent export interests in at least 8 of the 11 tables, followed by producers of cotton and coal (7 each), and softwood logs (5). Outside the area of agricultural products and raw materials, high-technology products—including aircraft, machinery, and scientific instruments—appear on most lists.

Even more important for our purposes, however, is what the tables tell us about the selective nature of export interests. For example, makers of aircraft sent 36 percent of their production abroad in 1976, but only 2 percent of their total output went to the countries that were the main potential targets of trade restriction on shoes in 1976 and 1977. On the other hand, 8 percent of their total production, and 21 percent of their exports, went to the major steel-exporting countries in 1976.

To take another example, these tables would suggest that soybean farmers had limited direct interest in the China textiles episode, and much more in those involving steel and cars. Wheat producers, by contrast, not only exported 68 percent of their production in 1982 but shipped almost 11 percent of that crop to China alone, the year before Beijing retaliated against textile quotas by slashing wheat purchases from the United States.

Has exporters' anti-protection activity in fact reflected the *intensity* of their trade interest, as measured here? In two important respects, it has.

First of all, over the past decade, major groups with high overall export dependence—the National Association of Wheat Growers (NAWG) and the American Soybean Association (ASA)—have greatly increased the time and money spent on international trade issues. The Wheat Growers have established a special, separately funded committee for this function.

The China textile case of 1983, moreover, suggests that their efforts varied according to their stakes. When Beijing sharply reduced purchases of US farm products in retaliation against US textile quotas, this provoked the NAWG, the most dependent sector, to mount a heavy campaign, seeking a compromise settlement of the textile dispute. Quite a few farmers sent letters; they brought in Senate Finance Committee Chairman Robert J. Dole (R-Kan.) to counter textile industry champions Strom Thurmond (R-SC) and Jesse Helms (R-NC). The soybean producers were less active, reflecting the fact that their sales had been declining and were very small by 1982. Similarly, other export groups dependent on the Chinese market, but less so than wheat, were affected less by the embargo and were not as active in US politics. Some of them did nothing at all.[20]

Interviews with experienced representatives of exporter organizations suggest that such behavior can reflect conscious, calculated strategy. When deciding whether or not to make a major political commitment, they pay attention to whether the restrictions will hit their particular foreign customers.

---

20. See appendix A for full activity lists.

If not, they are more likely to confine their activity to signing joint letters and the like.

The second way that exporter political activity reflected trade dependence is that it appears to have declined rather substantially as US foreign sales stagnated in the 1980s, and hence dropped as a share of total goods production. Exporters were major participants in the campaign against domestic content legislation in 1982–83, and (of course) the China textile episode of 1983. They were very minor players, however, in the footwear and Jenkins textile bill anti-protection campaigns of 1984–86.[21]

In some episodes, the relationship between trade dependence and activity appears mixed. Wheat growers were moderately active against the 1984 change in the textile rules of origin and the 1985 Jenkins bill, as well as earlier against auto domestic content. They signed joint letters opposing shoe protection in 1976 and 1981, while in 1985 they made a strong effort in the same cause. But they avoided involvement in sugar issues (as did exporters in general), and they confined their 1984 opposition to steel and copper protection to signing joint letters.

The American Soybean Association has been particularly aggressive on trade issues involving its major markets—the European Community and Japan. It mounted a strong attack on a 1984 legislative proposal to protect California wine producers, with an eye to the threat of EC retaliation against soybeans, and in so doing incurred the wrath of a prime sponsor, Representative Tony Coelho (D-Cal.). But the soybean lobby too makes an exception for sugar, even though the quota system has created the corn sweetener industry whose byproduct, corn gluten, competes directly with soybean meal, especially in Europe. (One reason is that soybean farmers often also grow corn.)

The largest and broadest agricultural organization, the American Farm

---

21. As a share of US goods production, exports (on a price-deflated basis) dropped from 13.9 to 10.3 percent between 1980 and 1985. Interestingly, anti-protection activity on our last seven episodes, from the domestic content to the Jenkins bill, followed a similar trend. Total activity ratings for exporters in those episodes were 67, 21, 14, 29, 6, 7,and 6, respectively; the numbers for exporters' share of total activity were .19, .40, .12, .09, .06, .04, and .02. See appendix A.

This striking trend is accentuated by the presence of the China textile episode second in this sequence, and our activity ratings offer just a rough measure, not a definitive indicator, when employed in this way. Nonetheless, the change is dramatic, and in the direction one would expect assuming a relationship between activity and trade dependence.

Bureau Federation, has long backed trade liberalization and has testified against protective measures like import surcharges and statutory quotas.[22] As a conglomerate organization, however, the Farm Bureau house contains some protectionist rooms as well, and so it has also backed protection for specialized products. It has opposed trade preferences for developing countries, and it objected to the Caribbean Basin Initiative on behalf of sugar and fruit and vegetable growers. The Farm Bureau opposes Japan's quotas on imports of beef, citrus, and other agricultural products, while supporting US meat import restrictions. We have not found any evidence of Farm Bureau opposition to product-specific protection in our episodes prior to the 1982–83 auto domestic content bill. In that case and in those dealing with copper and steel in 1984, the organization did join anti-protection coalitions, but confined its effort largely to attending meetings and signing letters. The National Grange, National Association of Farmer Cooperatives, and National Corn Growers Association have participated similarly in recent struggles. The Grange orchestrated a joint letter signed by many other organizations in response to the domestic content bill.

Cotton producers, backers of open trade policies for most of American history, have in the postwar period become supporters of textile protection and part of the lobbying coalition led by the American Textile Manufacturers Institute (ATMI). This is true even though 67 percent of their 1984 crop was exported, and 19 percent of it, $700 million worth, went to the Big Four exporters who were the Jenkins bill's prime targets. Cotton farmers evidently identify their greater interest with the domestic fabric and clothing makers, reasoning that, if they went under, US cotton exports to foreign countries would not rise equally. In addition, the National Cotton Council, the chief organization representing these farmers, includes domestic textile industry representatives as integral members. This suggests a broader proposition: that an exporter's anti-protection activity may be diminished if it also sells substantially to a US industry facing severe import competition.

This abstention from anti-protection activity has spilled over to other sectors. Although cotton producers are more dependent on sales to shoe-exporting countries than any other major export sector, they kept quiet during both footwear campaigns investigated here.

Among industrial exporters, Caterpillar, Inc., has been especially active

---

22. The Farm Bureau went on record against the 1981 Danforth auto quota bill, though it never reached the committee mark-up stage and was aimed mainly at getting Japan to restrain exports.

in trade politics. It gave particular lobbying priority in 1983–85 to the overvalued dollar, which undercut its competitiveness in third-country markets vis-à-vis firms like Komatsu of Japan. (So also did the Business Roundtable, within which Caterpillar executive Lee Morgan has been a leading force.) The National Electrical Manufacturers Association has generally been an anti-protection force (and was particularly active in the copper episode, as noted in the succeeding section of this chapter). But its trade position deteriorated very sharply in the early 1980s, and its commitment to liberal trade seems to have eroded somewhat as a consequence.

Notable for their relatively light anti-protection activity on product issues, in relation to their interest, have been the aircraft industry and the coal producers, especially the latter. The former supports an active Washington presence, and the CEOs of companies like Boeing have been personally engaged in support of liberal trade legislation. Their highest priority, however, has been to issues of export finance and subsidized foreign competitors like the European airbus. Coal producers and their union, the United Mine Workers, have largely kept quiet.

BUSINESS AND INDUSTRIAL IMPORT USERS

Products like steel, copper, raw sugar, or semiconductors are not, in the main, sold to household consumers. The main demand for them is business demand, from firms that use them as inputs to the products they market. Thus, we would expect activity to resist proposed import restrictions from those in the business community that benefit from the increased product availability and lower input prices that imports bring.

Overall, such products constitute around half of what Americans buy abroad. Imports of industrial supplies and materials were $109 billion in 1985, 32 percent of total imports. Capital goods, excluding autos, accounted for an additional $62.6 billion, or 19 percent.[23] In 1981, the percentage was even higher: these two categories totaled 65 percent of US imports, and over 50 percent if petroleum products are excluded from the calculation.[24]

It is not surprising, therefore, that user after user of Japanese electronic

---

23. *Survey of Current Business* (January 1986), table 4.3.
24. These percentages were calculated from figures in *Economic Report of the President,* February 1986, table B-100.

products—74 in all—flooded hearings at the Commerce Department in April 1987 to argue that the sanctions President Ronald Reagan had announced against Japan in the dispute over trade in semiconductors should not be imposed on products on which *they* depended. As with exporters, however, and as illustrated by this example, we would expect import-users' trade-political activity to be selective, with priority to protection-threatened products on which they are substantially dependent. Other things being equal, we would predict that the higher the cost share of an imported input[25] in a production group's output, the greater the anti-protection activity. This relationship should hold true even for firms that buy mainly from domestic suppliers, since import restrictions will increase the price they pay.

Our 14 episodes cover six products. Three of them are primarily producer goods: copper, steel, and sugar.[26] A look at input-output tables for each in the year 1977 (the most recent available) yields information on which domestic industries depend particularly on them as inputs for their production processes. Table 3.6 presents these results for copper (others are included in appendix B). Copper as an input, for example, contributes 25 percent or more of the output value of three industrial product categories, whose manufacture occupies over 120,000 workers. For steel, there are 20 such product lines above the 25 percent level, and these steel users employ nearly a million workers—not counting autos or auto parts. For sugar, dependence is weaker in straight input-output terms: no product except flavoring extracts has a coefficient significantly above the 10 percent level. But this is offset by the atypically great impact of current protection on that product's price: quotas keep out foreign sugar that could on the average be had for at least one-quarter below the current price, according to one careful estimate.[27]

Has import dependence plus protectionist threat then generated political action by user firms or associations representing them? In general, the answer is at least a qualified "yes": users were active, and increasingly so, in all of the episodes involving industrial inputs.[28]

---

25. As the surrounding discussion suggests, we use the phrase "imported input" as shorthand for a product (like steel) in which imports have a substantial share of the US market.
26. Two, autos and shoes, are sold principally to final consumers. One—textiles—is a mixed case, with fabric and yarn being mainly producer goods but apparel (three-fourths of the dollar total in 1984) being a household good.
27. Hufbauer, Berliner, and Elliott, pp. 294–95. The authors estimate, over the 1977–84 period, that import restrictions have induced an increase in the US price of sugar averaging 30 percent. The difference in 1987 is even greater as a result of subsequent reductions in quota levels.
28. For those products with more than one episode, there was also a trend for such activity to

TABLE 3.6 **Users of primary copper**[a]

I-O	SIC	Commodity	Copper coefficient	1983 employment (thousands)
38.0700	3351	Copper rolling and drawing	.542	25.5
38.1000	3357	Nonferrous wire drawing and insulating	.257	28.9
38.1200	3362	Brass, bronze, and copper castings	.255	14.1
38.0500	3339	Primary nonferrous metals n.e.c.	.249	9.0
38.0900	3356	Nonferrous rolling and drawing n.e.c.	.139	19.9[b]
37.0402	3399	Primary metal products n.e.c.	.132	10.7
40.0200	3432	Plumbing fixture fittings and trim	.113	24.4

I-O   input-output; SIC   Standard Industrial Classification; n.e.c.   not elsewhere classified.
Source: US Department of Commerce, *Detailed Input-Output Structure of the US Economy, 1977* Washington, 1984; US Department of Commerce, *Trade and Employment* TM-3-84, Washington, November 1984.
a. I-O 38.01, SIC 3331.
b. Includes SIC 3355, aluminum rolling and drawing, n.e.c.

The answer is clearly affirmative in the case of copper, whose users, represented by the National Electrical Manufacturers Association and the Copper and Brass Fabricators Council, actively and successfully resisted the copper producers' petition for escape clause relief in 1984. Their brief but intense campaign highlighted the direct costs of quotas to the fabricators, the resulting disadvantage they would face vis-à-vis foreign competitors, and the fact that copper-using industries employed (by conservative measurement) more than four times as many workers as the copper producers.

Sugar users have organized and appeared on the scene repeatedly: they

increase, absolutely and relative to that of other anti-protection actors. As a share of total activity, that by users in the sugar cases rose from .42 to .49 to .63; for steel the proportions were .27, .05, and .44. This probably reflected, in part, the increase in imports as a share of US domestic production, just as the fall-off in exporters' activity in the 1980s paralleled their *decline* in trade dependence. See appendix A for the underlying data.

were a moderately important force when the House of Representatives voted down Sugar Act renewal in 1974. Led by soft drink bottlers and ice cream makers, they deployed a major campaign to defeat new legislation in 1978 and 1979, and were moderately visible in the 1981 fight that they ultimately lost. Recently the Coalition to Resist Inflated Sugar Prices (CRISP), which combines user, consumer, refining and marketing interests, has been attacking the costs of the current tight quota regime.

For steel, the most important by far of the producer goods cases in terms of import value, the story is more complicated. On the anti-protection side, political activity has increased sharply, comparing the three episodes we have studied, and more has been going on than is often recognized. For instance, appendix A shows that in the 1984 episode, a long list of companies and associations went to the expense of testifying before the Senate, the House, and the USITC, or wrote letters to the President. But this activity still fell considerably short of the level that trade dependence and protectionist threat would indicate. Many other steel users have stayed on the sidelines, or even helped the other side.

A few fabricators testified in 1977 that they were concerned about the trigger price mechanism, although they often focused on specific items of concern to them, and coupled their remarks with pledges of concern about the welfare of the American steel industry. The 1982 avalanche of complaints about unfair foreign trade practices, which resulted in European export restraints, elicited virtually no observable opposition from US steel users.

Many of the product lines in the steel user table (table B.12) correspond to a producer political organization, such as the Industrial Fasteners Institute, the Can Manufacturers Institute, the Metal Building Dealers Association, the Spring Manufacturers Institute, the Metalstamping Association, the Construction Industry Manufacturers Association, and the National Screw Machine Products Association. Several of these joined forces a decade ago and created the Alliance of Metalworking Industries, composed of five associations representing 16,000 firms, many of them small.

Trade has become a priority issue for this Alliance in the 1980s. And when the steel industry pressed a three-pronged protection campaign, pushing a quota bill in Congress, an escape clause case with the USITC, and a large number of unfair trade cases, a few of its members did join with some other steel-using industrial groups in taking a formal stand in opposition. Those testifying against big steel in 1984 included the American Wire Producers Association, the Hack and Band Saw Manufacturers Association, and several nonintegrated US steelmakers. The hardware manufacturers association lobbied, the metal stamping association wrote a letter the to USTR, and most of the other metal-working associations passed resolutions—all these against import restrictions. Among the others who signed joint letters were producers of derricks, fences, construction machinery, springs, and pipe.

But as a general matter, steel-using interests as a group have been less active than their trade interests would seem to warrant. Several factors help account for this anomaly. Steel users are a very large group, and any large group suffers more from the free-rider problem in mobilizing on behalf of its interests. Many metalworking companies are tiny: unaccustomed to monitoring trade issues, lacking the resources to spend.

Steel is also a sector in which the unfair trade laws have been a prominent element in the political process. Interviews with Washington representatives of metalworking companies who do focus on international commerce give the impression that such firms tend to think of imports as, basically, something "bad." Those that profit from foreign-produced inputs do not wish to advertise the fact. And while user firms are increasingly concerned about import competition in their own output markets, this does not necessarily drive them to oppose steel quotas, or even to identify them as a major source of competitive disadvantage, as did the copper fabricators. Some are more inclined to seek protection for their own products.[29] Many metal stamping firms sell customized products to the aerospace industry, while another large group supplies the auto companies, and each subgroup may tend to identify its trade interest with that of its prime customer.[30]

Among large steel-using firms, Caterpillar, Inc., has been quite sensitive to the threat that trade restrictions would drive up input costs: it even argued against the auto domestic content bill on the grounds that it would reduce the efficiency of their own suppliers and increase labor costs.[31] In 1984, Caterpillar was unusually active in resisting steel quotas, billing itself as the second largest American steel user as well as the biggest exporter of US-

---

29. In theory, of course, a firm could actively seek open markets for its inputs and shelter for its outputs. While such a stand would be economically rational, it could be politically embarrassing and hard to sustain.

30. Firms can also, of course, respond economically to input prices by passing on increased costs to their buyers, or by moving production offshore. To the degree that these are viable options, producers are less likely to seek political action. For small firms, however, these options are difficult to pursue successfully.

31. Timothy L. Elder, Caterpillar, Inc. (US Congress, House, Ways and Means Subcommittee on Trade, Hearings on the Fair Practices in Automotive Products Act, 97th Cong., 2nd sess., 20, 21–24, 27–30 September 1982, Washington, p. 802).

made steel. Company representatives testified before the USITC, arguing that quotas would cost the company a great deal in product availability and quality as well as price, and pressed their case also with the administration and the Congress.

But interviews with Washington representatives of groups involved in this issue indicate that, in the 1984 steel case, efforts by private-sector leaders, such as Caterpillar and others, to build a broad, anti-protection coalition achieved very limited success.[32] West Coast users, particularly import-dependent because of their distance from the major domestic sources of supply, engaged counsel to argue before the USITC and the executive and legislative branches. General Electric testified before the USITC, but reportedly did not respond to urgings that it do more. We have found no evidence of significant activity by producers of steel furniture, many types of machinery, or—most important—automobiles. General Motors, a major steel user and consistent backer of open trade, did not get directly involved, notwithstanding the entreaties of more than one anti-protection activist. A major conglomerate and steel user declined because it owns a steel-producing subsidiary. A major oil company and user of steel pipe reportedly reached an agreement with US Steel not to work against protection. Two officials deeply involved in the 1984 steel episode each volunteered that the most intense user lobbying they remembered came after the quota decision, and that these interests sought not reversal of that decision but favorable treatment for their own imports within the restraint system. Just as exporters may direct their political resources only at selected targets where their stakes are concentrated, so may import users.

These specific tales suggest a broader ambivalence. Users may be dependent on imports, but they may also be dependent on their traditional suppliers. They may fear economic retaliation if they oppose their domestic suppliers; they may value their long-standing business ties; they may feel that foreign suppliers will disfavor them if the domestic industry is truncated. Even the activist copper fabricators were uncomfortable with fighting their domestic suppliers, as illustrated by their receptiveness, at least initially, when the producers proposed an international copper *production* restraint agreement aimed at protecting US users as well. Some large steel-using firms apparently had gentleman's agreements with steel industry executives; or they did not

---

32. The New York-based American Institute for Imported Steel sought to act as an umbrella organization for anti-protection interests in this case, but it represents importers, not users.

want to offend the steel companies who were their primary suppliers; or they did not want to get their unions angry by opposing protection; or they were seeking protection themselves or sold primarily to an industry that was.

This raises a final general question, one of downstream dependence. Who uses the steel users' products? The answer, as revealed by a further look at input-output data, is two predominant industry groupings: automobiles and construction. The former have, of course, been beneficiaries of their own protection in recent years. The latter, although it faces little direct import competition, should suffer from protection in the form of higher prices resulting in lower overall demand for its products and services. And it is, potentially, a major political force. The building construction industry employs 1.16 million workers; 764,000 more are engaged in heavy construction (bridges, roads, sewage systems). In addition, roughly 175,000 employees of steel-user firms are engaged in manufacture of inputs for building construction.

Steel can be a significant cost for this industry: it represents, for example, about 10 percent of the cost of new warehouses. (Another significant product on which it depends is lumber, whose cost has recently been rising as a result of an export tax imposed by Canada to avoid imposition by the United States of countervailing duties on imports.) But aside from Caterpillar, firms involved in or associated with construction have not been very evident in trade politics. Our data suggest they have an interest in becoming more involved.

RETAILERS

Retailers fall within the very important category of trade-related services, economic enterprises that finance, transport, and market both exports and imports. It is not hard to find examples of trade dependence elsewhere within this complex.

• Port communities also prosper according to the volume of trade, as do maritime interests.

• Importers have an obvious direct interest.

• Intranational transportation interests get much of their business from goods originating from, or destined for, other nations.

Most of these interests, however, have not been consistently active in trade politics. Many bankers recognize and talk about their trade dependence, and that of their developing-country clients, and a Bankers Association for Foreign Trade reflects this interest. But few senior bank executives have been willing to spend political capital to resist proposed specific import restrictions. US maritime interests ship only a fraction of American exports and imports, and give priority to inducing government to help them maintain or expand this market share rather than to maximizing overall trade volume.[33] Port interests have been involved on specific issues where they were threatened with substantial business losses; they were moderately active, for example, in the broad coalition that resisted the domestic content legislation. The national association of port authorities and the stevedore companies objected officially to the 1984 steel measures as well. The International Longshoremen's Association has appeared on the scene periodically, for instance opposing sugar quotas in 1978–79. Importers, represented by the recently renamed American Association of Exporters and Importers, have not hesitated to take anti-protection stands. But the most interesting service-sector group visible in recent trade battles, the one with the greatest political potential, is the retail business.

In calendar year 1985, US retail establishments employed 16.6 million Americans and sold nearly $1.5 trillion in merchandise. This included imports of manufactured consumer goods valued at $126 billion when they reached our borders, before internal distribution costs and retail markups were added.[34]

Retailers thus have major trade-related business. They also have deep roots in communities across the United States, hence a strong base from which to influence the national political process. But do they suffer severe pain from trade's curtailment? Skeptics argue the negative, contending that if imports are restricted, retail establishments will substitute domestic goods, raise their prices, and stay in business. There are at least three conditions, however, under which trade restrictions would impose serious economic costs:

(A) if a particular group of retailers sold primarily to a market niche for

---

33. In 1983, the US foreign trade fleet carried 16.1 percent of all US foreign trade by value and 5.8 percent by weight. Oceanborne foreign trade totaled $267.4 billion; US flag vessels transported $43.0 worth, carrying "a substantially greater portion of the high value liner commodities (27.2 percent) than of the low-value nonliner, dry bulk (1.7 percent) and tanker (6.8 percent) cargoes." (US Department of Commerce, *U.S. Industrial Outlook 1985*, Washington, 1985, p. 52-13.)

34. *Survey of Current Business* (March 1986), p. 87.

which imports were a large share of current supply, and domestic substitutes were only available in lesser quantity and at higher prices
(B) if the price elasticity of demand for a major product class were such that the higher prices caused by import restrictions would reduce sales volume substantially
(C) if import curbs were to be imposed quickly without warning, disrupting the delivery of goods already contracted from overseas sources.

To the degree that Condition A held, particular segments of the retail community, if not the entire group, would be natural leaders in anti-protection coalitions, since they would pay disproportionate costs from import restrictions. Conditions B and C would be expected to trigger broader resistance to trade restrictions, and general organizations representing retailers (like the American Retail Federation) might be expected to take the lead.

What light can our episodes shed on this question? Three of the products most prominent in recent US trade politics—automobiles, textiles, and footwear—are sold primarily through retail outlets to household consumers. (Most sugar goes first to industry.) It is these outlets that have a stake in final-product imports parallel to that of manufacturers in intermediate-goods imports.

The marketing of these products is big business. To cite some statistics drawn from retailer sources, the National Automobile Dealers Association (NADA) reported total employment at new car dealerships at 695,700 in the recession year of 1982, as the domestic content bill was gathering steam.[35] Footwear accounted for approximately 307,400 jobs at the retail level in 1984, more than twice as many jobs as footwear manufacturing employment (115,000). For apparel, sold heavily through department store and discount chains, retail employment has been estimated at 2,100,000.[36] And, as appendix A shows, we found retailers to be active on the anti-protection side on all of the episodes involving these products.

Are there specific segments of the retail community that are particularly dependent on imports? Neither companies nor the Census Bureau collect

---

35. NADA Data, reported in Department of Commerce, *Statistical Abstract of the United States* (Washington, 1985), table no. 1410.
36. The estimates for footwear and apparel retailing jobs are based on data from the National Retail Merchandising Association ("Merchandising and Operating Results of Department and Specialty Stores," 1976 and 1984, New York), and Bureau of Labor Statistics, *Employment and Earnings, United States, 1907–78,* and *Supplement,* 1984 and 1986.

merchandise sales data on the basis of where goods originate, so there is no precise way to determine the import-dependence of particular stores or retailer groups. There are clearly categories of stores, however, that sell particularly high proportions of imports. This is a result of the increasing differentiation among large retail establishments in the decades since World War II, and especially the emergence of chains (such as K-Mart, Zayre's, and Pay-Less Shoes) catering to lower income customers.

Their strategies for attracting these customers depend on filling their shelves with low-priced goods, and increasingly the buyers for these chains find that such goods cannot be supplied from domestic sources. So not only do they go overseas, they even develop prototype products and then find a foreign firm (a Brazilian shoe producer, for example) to do mass manufacturing to their specifications. Thus, some retailers have indeed placed their bets on a specialized competitive strategy that, they feel, is quite vulnerable to import curbs.

Footwear offers, in fact, a particularly strong example of a substantial and concentrated retailer interest in maintaining foreign sources of supply. In 1984, imports "accounted for about 71 percent of apparent US consumption" by volume, and 54 percent by value.[37] As these statistics show, imports are concentrated in the lower end of the price range. The major marketers of these imports are the "volume retailers," stores for which shoes are the sole or primary business, and which sell large numbers of relatively standardized products at economical prices. Thus, although the retail community in general is a huge group, the costs of shoe protection fall especially on a small subset, which reduces the collective action problem.

Their trade association, the Footwear Retailers of America, has been in business for decades, and has grown increasingly active as its members' import-dependence has increased. In the 1976–77 shoe episode, this association (then called the Volume Footwear Retailers of America) testified, commissioned studies on the impact of proposed restrictions, and lobbied to some extent, but they did not manage a "full-court press." According to interview sources active on this issue, however, FRA political activity was heavy indeed in the political struggle culminating in the 1985 shoe case. The

---

37. USITC, *Nonrubber Footwear*, USITC Publication No. 1717, July 1985, pp. A19, A25. Stores that carry mainly shoes account for 64.4 percent (by value) of total footwear sales in the United States. (Department of Commerce, *1982 Census of Retail Trade: Industry Series Merchandise Line Sales*, RC82-1-3, Washington, p. 3-23.)

Washington office mounted a sustained effort to convey information—to the USITC, the Congress, and the executive branch—about the contemporary US shoe business, the growing role of imports in that business, and the abandonment of many product lines by US manufacturers who were not cost-competitive. The organization commissioned studies on the cost of trade restrictions to consumers per job saved. In 1985, the USITC nonetheless recommended rather stringent quota protection, in response to a petition by the Footwear Industry Association of America that was backed by influential members of the Senate Committee on Finance. The shoe stores responded by pushing the administration and congressional allies as well. Delegations of shoestore managers met with senators. Focusing primarily on Republican senators from the West, the FRA and its allies persuaded 19 senators to sign a letter to the President urging him to reject footwear protection. Insiders report that the campaign was not only heavy but also sophisticated in political technique.

There is a similar concentration of interest among automobile retailers. In 1982, 4,000 dealerships sold only imports. These were local businesses that meant jobs for their communities, and they were organized by manufacturer (for example, Toyota Motor Sales, Inc.) as well as generally in the American International Auto Dealers Association (AIADA). These dealers, with financial backing from Toyota, Honda, and others, were the ground troops of the coalition opposing the domestic content bill in 1982 and 1983. They were reinforced by the existence of 7,250 other dealers who sold both domestic and imported makes.[38] And many operators of the 56 percent of dealerships that were purely domestic also owned foreign car outlets. Profits from these outlets had kept no small number of them afloat in the early 1980s during the lean years for GM, Ford, and Chrysler. Not wishing to kill this golden goose, the general trade association for all car retailers, the National Auto Dealers Association, joined the AIADA in taking a stand against domestic content.

Imported apparel, by contrast, is sold mainly by stores that also sell other products. So Condition A (above) holds to a lesser degree than it does for cars or shoes. But Conditions B and C have been highly relevant. Concerning the first, an Institute study estimates that domestic apparel production would

---

38. Thus, there were 11,250 dealers for whom imports were all or part of their car business, compared to 14,450 who sold domestic brands only. Data taken from NADA Data, Department of Commerce, *Statistical Abstract of the United States*, 1985.

make up less than half of the volume reduction in apparel imports that would have come from enactment of the Jenkins bill.[39] A study prepared for the retailers, which reached even more drastic conclusions, estimated that the resulting drop in domestic consumption, would cost the apparel retailing business some 58,000 jobs.[40] Condition C also held for apparel in 1984. The Department of Commerce announced in August that "country of origin" rules would be tightened as of October, posing the threat that stores would not be able to fill orders already contracted for the decisive Christmas season. This was a powerful catalyst in energizing the Retail Industry Trade Action Coalition (RITAC), representing major chain stores and trade associations, to launch a counterattack against trade restrictions, primarily in the textile-apparel arena. The umbrella retailer organizations—the American Retail Federation and the National Retail Merchants Association—had long been general supporters of open trade, but the sudden textile tightening intensified their concerns. As one representative long associated with retailers noted in an interview, "It is death for a buyer to be cut off from too many product sources," and not be able to fill the shelves with products fitting his store's market niche.

The RITAC story further illustrates the upsurge in, and limits to, retailers' trade-political activity. Created in June 1984, primarily on the initiative of the Dayton Hudson Corporation of Minneapolis and its chief executive officer, William A. Andres, the organization reflected the increased import-dependence of department stores, and the fear of their managements that textile protectionism would make them unable to offer customers a full range of clothing and accessories at attractive prices. Member companies included K-Mart, Zayre's, J. C. Penney, Macy's, Sears, Carter Hawley Hale, Federated, Ward, and all the major retail associations. RITAC raised approximately $600,000 from member companies for its first-year budget, reportedly the most the retail establishment had ever allocated to any public policy campaign. It got its baptism of fire in winning a delay in implementation and slight modification of the substance of the new "country-of-origin" rules for the textile quota system proposed by the Reagan administration in the summer of 1984. By all accounts, however, RITAC's effectiveness as an anti-

---

39. William R. Cline, *The Future of World Trade in Textiles and Apparel* (Washington: Institute for International Economics, 1987).

40. Laura Megna Baughman and Thomas Emrich, "Analysis of the Impact of the Textile and Apparel Trade Enforcement Act of 1985," International Business and Economic Research Corporation, June 1985, table 4.

protection force was limited that fall by tensions within the retail community, among the existing trade associations, and between them and the RITAC staff.

In early 1985, RITAC was brought under the wing of one of the two major trade associations, the American Retail Federation. It immediately confronted a stiffer challenge from the textile-apparel complex in the form of the "Jenkins bill," which would have rolled back textile and apparel imports substantially: those from the three major exporters would have dropped by an average of 30 percent.[41] This was so restrictive that it was easy to show retail executives its substantial money costs to their businesses. This made it a near-perfect catalyst for mobilizing anti-protection activity.

In the beginning, no one, including retailers, took the Jenkins bill very seriously as a legislative threat. But as the number of House cosponsors approached 300, and the Reagan administration was slow to respond, the retailers organized in opposition. By May, RITAC had collected, from their 1985 dues and a special emergency assessment, a war chest of $2,000,000 to fight the bill. This was spent on grass-roots lobbying—including appeals to store customers and employees—and Washington organizing and coalition-building. By summer, Capitol Hill was beginning to notice. One member of Congress told the authors in July 1985: "I just started getting letters from the employees of department stores saying that the [textile] bill will hurt them. This is the first time I've seen anything like this—a batch of hand-written letters, apparently from clerks." An independent coalition of California firms also formed their own American Free Trade Council, which announced that they were spending another $500,000 to stop the bill.[42]

When the textile industry pushed for enactment of the bill in its original form, retailers worked with the administration and other interest-group representatives—including those working for foreign suppliers—to "peel off" the least-committed of the bill's supporters. RITAC and its allies thus claimed victory when about 30 fewer members voted for the bill than had cosponsored it, and because the substantial House margin the textile industry

---

41. See Cline, ch. 9. The original House bill would have rolled back imports from the top 12 foreign suppliers. It was modified in the Senate so that the harshest provisions would have applied only to the top three suppliers, softening the blow to fourth-ranked China, which had retaliated over textile quotas two years earlier.

42. At one point they tried distributing hundreds of teddy bears in Washington, making the point that higher prices would "ruin Christmas" for many moderate-income families. (*New York Times*, 24 September 1985.)

still won, 262–159, was 19 votes shy of what would be required to override a presidential veto. RITAC developed in the process an argument, repeated by members in floor debate, that it would cost the nation more jobs in apparel retailing than it would create in apparel manufacturing.[43] They continued to be actively involved as the bill passed the Senate and was vetoed by the President in 1985, and when the textile quota advocates failed by eight votes to override the veto the following summer.

On balance, RITAC made a substantial—though limited—mark on trade politics. It was designed as a short-run operation. It engaged a number of corporate CEOs, but it was predominantly a Washington-based, staff-directed enterprise, in contrast to the opposition American Textile Manufacturers Institute where the CEOs clearly call the shots. This reflects a continuing asymmetry of interest: the trade stakes of mass market retailers, while substantial, are of a lesser order of magnitude. It reflects also, partly for this reason, a much younger and weaker tradition of collective political action on trade, and the uneasy coexistence of such action with the fierce commercial rivalries that characterize the retail business. And it reflects the fact that the political orientation of retail executives tends to be local, not national, aimed at strengthening community ties (and bringing in customers) while avoiding controversial policy stands that might drive them away.

Still, if the tide of retailer trade activism seems likely to recede, it seems unlikely to drop back to the pre-RITAC level. A number of corporate leaders and staff aides have been educated and sensitized to their dependence on a permissive national trade policy climate. The fact that the Jenkins bill did not become law—that retail activists could claim some return on the political investment, even facing one of the toughest lobbies in town—is important as well in encouraging future activity.

---

43. The Baughman and Emrich study showed 58,000 apparel retailing jobs lost, as opposed to 36,000 apparel manufacturing jobs gained. The pro-protection side, not surprisingly, was predicting a much higher job gain: 947,000 jobs saved in textiles and apparel manufacturing through 1990, and 1.89 million in the economy as a whole. Also not surprisingly, the retailers were selective in choosing which data to highlight. They did not emphasize their study's conclusion that for textiles alone, and for textiles plus apparel, retail jobs lost as a result of the Jenkins bill would be fewer than producer jobs gained. See Cline, ch. 9, for a comparison of the various estimates.

TARGETED COUNTRIES' EXPORTERS AND GOVERNMENTS

In product-specific trade episodes, the trend in anti-protection effort was upward not only for special-interest US groups, our main subject, but also for companies and governments from other countries. Reckoned in the same rough way used for domestic actors, activity of foreign interests increased comparably in the last seven cases (beginning with autos 1982–83): it was about three times as great, on average, as in the first seven episodes. The causes of their increased activity probably included some of the same conditions driving domestic actors, especially increased dependence on the US market, and a greater threat to their trade interests, or threats to larger sectors, than before. In addition, the general explosion of lobbying and trade law in Washington probably induced foreign, as well as domestic, clients to decide they could not afford to be left out. More individual companies from abroad, such as Hyundai and Samsung of Korea, are following the example of US companies and establishing their own Washington offices, independent of their embassies.

On trade issues, foreign firms and governments use political tactics similar to those used by American groups in some respects, ranging from the minimal to the large-scale campaign. It is quite legal in the United States for foreign groups to make known how they would be affected and what measures they prefer, in advance of decisions by Congress or the USITC, as long as their representatives are registered publicly as foreign agents. Our activity ratings reflect their public testimony and statements on many occasions.

But their alien status does, of course, make a political difference. For one thing, the "foreign" label is a distinct disadvantage. So efforts out in the open to rally mass American opinion risk goading the opposition even more, and hence may be less attractive than private contacts with officials. Indeed, until recently, most governments avoided even private lobbying of US officials, apart from the State Department.

There has clearly been an increase in direct lobbying in the 1980s, due above all to trade issues. But lacking citizenship and the vote, foreign groups still tend to rely relatively less on direct presentations to the government than the typical domestic interest group does. Some try to work indirectly as well, by attempting to activate and persuade specific, organized private US groups to express the same policy position to their own government. In 1984, Pinochet's Chile largely stayed in the background of the opposition to copper quotas, though their efforts there were extensive. In the foreground were the

American wire manufacturers who use copper inputs. In 1985 South Koreans carefully contacted US farm groups who sell in Korea, and pressed them to help by speaking against shoe import restrictions.[44] (In that case, farmers took little action on shoes that we were able to discover.) In 1985 the People's Republic of China wrote to some fifty chief executives of major US companies asking their assistance in opposing the Jenkins textile bill.

Financing is sometimes contributed also. Japanese car companies hired a small army of law firms and consultants in 1981 and 1982 to report on and try to influence the political process on auto import barriers. The greatest potential advantage of foreign players in this political process, however, is that they can credibly raise the threat of retaliation against US exports or investments overseas in order to discourage measures they oppose.

In the sugar 1974 episode, we found no foreign efforts to oppose or reduce protection. Officially the issue was renewal of the existing restrictive system, which allocated specific quotas to foreign suppliers, giving them assured access to high US prices. After living within the quota system for some forty years, they probably considered removal of US sugar import restraints to be most unlikely before it fell in their laps. And then they were not enthusiastic, fearing the loss of their price and market share guarantee more than hoping for increased US sales. But in all cases involving other products we find at least moderately strong opposing activity by some overseas actors.

Among our 14 episodes, the first instance of heavy foreign anti-protection effort was the vigorous 1982 opposition by the European Community (EC) to new steel import restrictions. In each case after that one, parties from other countries also waged a major campaign to stop new protection. Threats of retaliation have become fairly regular tools of international trade bargaining. In the 1984 steel episode, the EC, Canada, and even Korea all threatened retaliation at one stage or another. Just before President Reagan's decision, Ottawa's Trade Minister announced that Canada had prepared a product "hit list" in case action was taken against Canada.

In the end, Canada was exempted, the others were not, and no one retaliated. The People's Republic of China actually embargoed US products in the 1983 textile dispute, and Beijing threatened retaliation in the textile battles of 1984 and 1985. Hong Kong's textile industry in 1984 established what they described as a "multi-million dollar fighting fund," threatened court challenges against the new rules of origin, and took the United States

---

44. Interviews with participants in both campaigns.

to the General Agreement on Tariffs and Trade (GATT). Some private companies also called for a boycott of US cigarettes.

Summing Up

Something new happened in American trade politics between the mid-1970s and the mid-1980s: a marked increase in anti-protection political activity, at least in cases concerning specific products. The interests that have led the way have not been the general-interest coalition organizations or the traditional allies of liberal trade, the multinational corporations. Rather, they have been economic groups with more concentrated trade interests: exporters, import users, and retailers in the United States; and foreign governments and firms.

These groups were subject to the most immediate costs of recent US import barriers, and they responded by taking political action. There were cases of mixed interests—import users vulnerable to pressure from their domestic suppliers—and anomalies—groups like coal producers or construction interests whose stakes suggest greater involvement than has been evident in their practice. Important also have been the influence of such ancillary factors as certain groups' political traditions: the shoe retailers are more accustomed to collective anti-protection action than are the general retail establishments that market most imported clothing.

However, while probing the details of a particular episode, or the circumstances of a specific group, it is not easy to see the broad picture—the full range of forces that may have cut across different groups in the same way. It is also difficult to assess which factors mattered and which merely coincided with political activity. The future will present combinations of circumstances different from those in the period studied here, so it would be helpful if one could isolate the general conditions in which anti-protection activity will be the greatest (or the least), and the specific factors that might influence it, whatever the group to be assessed. The next chapter, therefore, develops a more comprehensive analysis of anti-protection political activity.

4 Opposition to Protection: General Sources and Limits

Granted that it is the *special* anti-protection interest groups that have been most active in resisting proposed trade restrictions, and granted that their activity increased markedly from the mid-1970s through the mid-1980s, what were the particular forces that drove specific groups into the political arena? Why, in a given episode, were certain groups heavily engaged while others stayed on the sidelines? And in general, under what conditions is this opposition likely to be greatest, and when will it be weakest?

This chapter develops a general analysis of the sources and limits of anti-protection activism by trade-affected interests. Two conditions appear to be primary in determining the extent of a group's political opposition: trade dependence, and a political threat to that interest. Several secondary conditions also contribute to anti-protection activity and its variations, across industries and across time. Among these are macroeconomic conditions; microeconomic characteristics of import-using industries beyond their trade dependence; the extent and form of industry political organization; and the tactics used by other participants in the trade-political process.

This chapter explores these apparent relationships, employing a mix of different types of evidence. The arguments developed here are based partly on contrasting examples presented in this chapter or earlier in this book, and partly on the findings of previous studies. But such evidence has its limits: general conclusions based only on selected examples cannot be regarded as final. As a supplement, therefore, half of these relationships are also subjected to more general econometric tests, in order to provide a different vantage point that helps offset the disadvantages of the other approaches. The latter evidence is summarized here and discussed in fuller, more technical detail in appendix C.[1]

---

1. Appendix C details our assumption, models, data, and results. In brief, each group found to be active in any of the 14 episodes is a member of a pool of observations. Also added are groups expected to be active on that product—for example, user industries for which the import

These statistical estimates, and the data that form their base, are both first ventures into relatively uncharted waters, and they are presented here in an experimental spirit. Some but not all tests provide strong support; tentative negative as well as positive results are reported. The results are not refined enough to provide a sole basis for confident conclusions; further statistical work would be necessary in order to verify the apparent findings. Ultimately, evidence of this type, too, will be insufficient by itself.

Two Primary Conditions

An obvious condition for anti-protection political activity of the sort we are investigating is some group dependence on trade. A second obvious condition for opposition activity is some threat to such trade interest: hence, anti-protection activity has expanded in reaction to the spread of political campaigns for protection.

TRADE DEPENDENCE

As spelled out in the previous chapter, foreign trade has become very big business to special interests that benefit from it, and these groups are increasingly sensitive to their trade interests. The groups most likely to act are those for whom foreign trade matters the most. In addition to heavy business users of imports, these include producers that export a substantial part of their output, and service interests, like retailers, relying on the inflow of foreign products. In addition, trade would have to matter to them in the sense that a disruption would impose costs on them. The greater their dependence on the trade in question and the greater the cost of protection that would reach them, the greater their anti-protection activity, and vice versa, other things being equal.

Many examples illustrate this relationship. As discussed in the previous chapter, wheat exporters were more dependent on the Chinese market than

---

is more than 25 percent of its output value—but which in fact remained inactive. A rating scheme is developed to provide a rough measure of the degree of activity for each group in each episode. Then, using the multinomial logit technique, we estimate the parameters of a model with the degree of activity as an ordinal dependent variable, and other variables, such as the group's dependence on the trade at issue, as explanatory variables. The number of observations for which trade-dependence data are complete is 292.

soy farmers during the 1983 textile dispute, and while Beijing's retaliation targeted exports of both, the National Wheat Growers Association brought much greater political pressure for a settlement. When trade protection could affect Japan and the European Communities (EC), however, on whose markets soy producers are much more dependent, it is the American Soybean Association that is heard loud and clear. In the copper case of 1984, electrical manufacturers depended far more on the trade at issue than users like the auto industry and the wheat exporters, and the former group was far more active politically.

There are always exceptions, of course, and a tentative econometric test of this relationship in general does not provide clear confirmation. The dependence effect has the expected sign but is not statistically significant (see appendix C). The apparent weakness in this case, however, could be a product of the way this sample was constructed; it is probably biased against finding a strong relation. The sample excludes all the many sectors having little dependence on the specific product trade at issue, permitting us to examine the relation only among those arrayed along the high end of the dependence dimension. If the least dependent also spend the least to oppose protection on that product, then adding them here would produce a stronger statistical relationship.

Trade dependence or economic internationalization could increase political opposition to protection not only in direct dealings with government, but also in activity by firms within their own industries. As the world economy has developed toward more complex specialization, some US industries have become more differentiated, into one set of firms specializing in trade and foreign investment, and others that are more domestically oriented. In several industries, the more internationally oriented firms have worked actively to block or dilute protective proposals pushed by their fellow producers. For example, the US shoe industry was, for a long time, highly oriented to the home market and highly unified. But divisions developed in the late 1970s, as several large companies began producing abroad or importing from foreign makers. When the "voluntary" restraint agreements with Korea and Taiwan expired in 1981, these big firms worked actively to undermine the shoe industry association's petition to have the restrictions extended. In several other industries as well, more externally oriented firms have worked actively to block or dilute protective proposals made by other firms.[2]

---

2. Helen Milner, "Resisting the Protectionist Temptation" (Ph.D. dissertation, Harvard University, Cambridge, Mass., 1986). Other producer groups marked by internal divisions at

Looking to the years ahead, we can expect that anti-protection activity will reflect future trends in specific groups' trade dependence: as the composition of exports and imports changes, patterns of political engagement will shift with them; if the US economy becomes more exposed internationally, aggregate opposition to protection will rise, other things being equal. If the merchandise trade deficit drops sharply or disappears, this will presumably involve today's import-related interests reducing their dependence on foreign goods, or export-related firms selling more abroad, or both. We would then expect political activity by export-related interests to increase relative to activity by import-related interests.

PRESSURE FOR PROTECTION

The impetus for groups to enter politics on trade issues will come from the belief that if they did nothing, public policy would impose burdens on them. A group will enter politics when a political threat to its trade interests appears, and it will act more vigorously in proportion to the strength of the challenge. This proposition is consistent with much of the experience surveyed in chapter 3, such as Caterpillar, Inc., resisting steel restraints in 1984 and mass-market retailers mobilizing against the Jenkins bill in 1985–86. It is consistent also with E. E. Schattschneider's generalizations about group political activity 27 years ago. Schattschneider maintains that pressure politics is often begun by a business group that is losing in private, economic competition with other segments of business. But when one side goes into politics, it necessarily enlarges the scope of the formerly private conflict, and this generally brings additional parties into the struggle, with effects that are difficult to predict.[3]

If the future should bring less pro-protection pressure in the aggregate, aggregate opposition will naturally decline. If barriers should be reduced, or in the absence of new protection efforts, or when these lack substantial

---

some point include automobiles, semiconductors, television sets, and apparel. Given its emphasis on episodes leading to government decision, our analysis has not focused directly on anti-protection activity within industry organizations. The subject clearly merits further study, however. For individual firms, such activity may often be less expensive, and more effective, than activity directed at the government.

3. *The Semisovereign People* (New York, NY: Holt, Rinehart, and Winston, 1960). This study does not include any "cases" in which a protection threat is absent, and has not attempted to measure degrees of threat.

political support, trade-dependent companies and organizations will shift their political resources toward other priorities. But even if the frequency of protection-seeking campaigns were to diminish, anti-protection activity would not necessarily be lighter in those episodes that did occur.

Secondary Influences

Given a relatively high degree of trade dependence and a threat thereto, we sometimes see less, and sometimes more, political effort against protection than we would expect from considering just these two variables. Several other influences help explain why.

MACROECONOMIC CONDITIONS: INFLATION AND THE DOLLAR

Changes in variables like inflation or the value of the dollar could have various impacts on anti-protection activity. They could be important indirectly, through their influence on trade-dependence, pro-protection threats, or both. (They could also directly shape the attitudes of government officials, regardless of interest group activity; that issue is treated in chapter 5.) It is less clear how they might have a *direct* impact on the degree of opposition to proposed restrictions.

Inflation

One frequent view holds that an acceleration of inflation, other things equal, should anger consumers and perhaps business as well, and that this should lead to stronger action against import barriers that raise prices.[4] During slower inflation, groups would find other problems more urgent than prices and protection, and hence complain less.

In battles over sugar import quotas, there is some evidence of inflation producing this effect: in all three cases examined here, sugar prices shot

---

4. This idea appears in various studies, such as Stephen P. Magee and Leslie Young, "Endogenous Protection in the United States, 1900–1984" (*US Trade Policies in a Changing World Economy*, edited by Robert M. Stern, Cambridge, Mass.: MIT Press, 1987), p. 150.

upward and certain consumer groups were quite active. But a preliminary econometric test based on data from across our 14 episodes does not confirm the conventional expectation. This may be because this argument assumes that the most affected groups are already organized—or will be induced to organize. Later we argue that such an assumption is dubious, although the organizational reality is changing.

Interestingly, what appendix C does report is that in the largest sample, faster inflation is associated statistically with less, rather than more, political opposition by the average group. Conceivably, higher inflation could make consumers less likely to resist specific price increases, and/or make it easier for import users to pass higher costs through to their buyers. More likely, perhaps, the econometric result is a reflection of variables that are omitted from this preliminary test. In the period of this study, relatively faster inflation coincided with lesser pro-protection pressures, and slower inflation with the spread of trade-restrictive campaigns. The pro-protection pressure appears to have generated increased anti-protection activity in response, but since we have not developed comparable measures for the pro-protection side, we could not include this in our models. Nor could we explore another plausible explanation: that both were influenced by the combination of tight monetary and loose fiscal policy that contributed to the strong dollar and the trade imbalance.[5]

The Dollar

Another macroeconomic dimension that could drive more interest groups to seek import protection, in turn inducing more political resistance, is a rising

---

5. It is also interesting to speculate that faster US inflation will change the relative trade dependence of US sectors, and hence their political activity. Faster inflation, relative to that abroad, should reduce US exporters' sales abroad, if the nominal exchange rate remains constant. The reduced dependence on trade relative to home markets should then make them less willing to expend political resources on export-related issues. Faster relative inflation would have the opposite effect on US buyers or retailers of imports, shifting them toward greater relative dependence on foreign goods, and hence greater political activity. We are grateful to Robert E. Baldwin for suggesting this relationship. During the last decade when anti-protection activity was rising in the aggregate, however, US inflation did not fluctuate much relative to the rest of the world. This suggests that other influences on trade dependence may have been more important during this period.

real exchange rate. A higher dollar, other things equal, would increase import competition and, generally, generate requests for political help from more sectors, while a dollar decline would reduce the demand for protection (again abstracting from other sources of competitive advantage). The exchange rate surely seems to have been a significant reason for the increased aggregate protection pressure during the 1980s.

Ideally, this two-step relation could be checked empirically with a two-sided simultaneous study. But lacking measures of pro-protection activity itself, one could at least determine whether exchange-rate changes correlate positively with anti-protection effort at the level of the individual group. An econometric estimate from recent episodes is in fact consistent with this idea. The relationship seems both positive and significant. Since the highest dollar observations came in the most recent years, however, this result may also reflect other variables which changed over this time: for example, organized capacity for group action has expanded enormously since the early 1970s.[6]

MICROECONOMIC INFLUENCES: IMPORT USERS AND IMPORT COMPETITION

It would be sensible to suppose that commercial interests will spend more resources on political activity when their own business is doing poorly, other things being equal. They would be expected to stick to business as long as it was going well. Various studies of pro-protection pressure have investigated whether industries are more likely to seek import restrictions when their work forces, output, or profits are falling, and when their import competition is rising. Eventually, a full study of the anti-protection side might also probe whether good times in their own sectors also make trade-dependent sectors more relaxed about trade politics, other things being equal, and whether bad times for exporters, import users, and the like—for whatever reason—make them more willing to expend political effort.

One of the more interesting microeconomic questions is the political effect

---

6. As with inflation, the dollar might affect anti-protection groups more directly. A real exchange rate appreciation could undermine the exporter's competitiveness and trade dependence, while swelling the import-related group's stake in trade, with opposite effects on their political behavior, at least if they assume these currency changes will endure. Beyond inflation and exchange rates, other macroeconomic dimensions, such as aggregate unemployment, may also shape the broad trade-political environment.

of import penetration on competing US producers who themselves use imported inputs in production. Such an increase in foreign competition might make a producer more sensitive to its own costs, and hence drive it to intensify its political opposition to protection for its inputs, as a means of containing costs and protecting its own competitiveness. Cane sugar refiners illustrated this response in 1978–79 and 1981–82, as did copper fabricators in 1984.

There are, however, alternative means of cost reduction. Some import users may decide instead to move production overseas where they will have access to cheaper inputs. Other user firms may emphasize commercial responses other than cost reduction, such as differentiating themselves from their competitors by changing the product, the marketing approach, or the after-sale service system. Still others may withdraw from some segments of their market in order to specialize more narrowly. Finally, some may decide to accept the cost of protection on their inputs, calculating that it will help them in the politics of seeking protection of their own, as auto producers did in 1980.[7]

In short, increasing import competition could cause a firm either to intensify its opposition to protection for its inputs, or provoke other economic and political responses. A preliminary general test with import users in recent product episodes suggests that, other things equal, greater import penetration significantly increases anti-protection effort (appendix C).[8]

DEGREE AND FORM OF INDUSTRY POLITICAL ORGANIZATION

The need to turn to politics is one thing; the capacity to act politically is another. Some broad features of political organization weaken anti-protection

---

7. Logically, such a user could work simultaneously against protection for its suppliers, but doing so would alienate potential political allies who will usually be needed in order to influence the government. So this response to import competition is likely to reduce user anti-protection activity, as it did in the auto case. Our sample is 113 user observations from all episodes. In general, the anti-protection effect seems to have dominated the other responses, at least during this period.

8. On the other hand, low price elasticity of demand might diminish an import user's political effort below that of others with the same trade dependence. The lower the elasticity of demand for its own products, the easier it will be for a firm to pass the costs of protection on downstream to its customers. If this response is available, the firm may choose it over an expensive political campaign to hold down its input costs.

efforts, while other US trends and circumstances may operate in the opposite direction.

Diffusion of Interest

The very size of potential anti-protection coalitions paradoxically may be a disadvantage, if it reduces the degree to which they organize permanently or mobilize during a given occasion below the level that would be optimal for their own interests. It is often argued that the larger the underlying group, and the more equal its members, the less will be the incentive of any member family or firm to contribute to an effort undertaken in its own interest, if this type of activity produces a collective good. That is, if one firm's or family's joining or abstaining will have little noticeable effect, and if it will enjoy the benefits of any campaign whether or not it helps pay the cost, then a self-interested player would refuse to finance lobbying and other activity on its own behalf. The most obvious player in our study fitting this description is the individual or household, considered as a member of the enormous group of shoe consumers, for instance. As seen in chapter 3, groups of consumers notoriously fail to spend much on political organizations or campaigns to advance their consumer interests in international trade.

But the free-rider problem is actually less of a barrier to anti-protection campaigns than is sometimes thought. Gains from anti-protection activity are not distributed evenly across the population; typically a much smaller set of actors stands to reap a disproportionate share of the gain from continuation of open trade. Moreover, for a smaller group, the individual's decision to participate has a bigger effect on whether the group acts or not, and the member reaps a larger share of the gain. Thus, in smaller and less equal groups the theoretical free-rider problem is mitigated, and actual collective action is likely to rise closer to the optimal level for the group's interests. Many contemporary industries satisfy this "small number solution" to the free-rider problem, at least as regards their common interests as producers of similar goods.[9]

---

9. Mancur Olson, *The Logic of Collective Action: Public Goods and the Theory of Groups* (Cambridge, Mass.: Harvard University Press, 1965), p. 143; George J. Stigler, "Free Riders and Collective Action: An Appendix to Theories of Economic Regulation," *Bell Journal of Economics*, vol. 5 (Autumn 1974), pp. 359–65.

Indeed, a central premise of this study is that while open trade may be, in important respects, a "public good," it is also a private good to important interests. So "anti-protection" is not always a fully public or collective good. The more narrowly a group defines the type of imported products it fights for, the more it channels the benefits of the anti-protection "good" to particular parties and excludes other possible beneficiaries. For example, as noted in the previous chapter, certain steel users were not very active against steel quotas in 1984, but spoke out loud and clear against restrictions on particular specialized steel items they needed for their own operations. The free-rider problem or other factors reduce political activity in some sectors below levels that might be expected from trade dependence, but limited activity also emerges through this constriction of the target.

We have not undertaken a quantitative test of this free-rider idea for explaining the level of anti-protection activity. One previous study, as well as indirect tests regarding pro-protection activity, have not been especially encouraging.[10] But the idea does suggest intuitively reasonable interpretations for some contrasts in our evidence. For instance, in footwear protection episodes, we find little activity by the consuming public as a whole, but vigorous activity, especially in 1985, by the shoe retailers' organization. Industrial users of copper are a much smaller group than users of steel, and political activity by the copper users was probably closer to the theoretical optimum than in the cases involving steel users.

---

10. Thomas A. Pugel and Ingo Walter reason that larger companies will be more active in support of trade liberalization legislation and in opposition to measures like the Burke-Hartke bill of 1971. But their survey of 68 firms found no support for this form of the hypothesis. "U.S. Corporate Interests and the Political Economy of Trade Policy," *Review of Economics and Statistics,* vol. 67 (August 1985), p. 471. Several other studies have attempted to find an effect of a pro-protection sector's concentration on that industry's level of official protection. Such a test focusing not directly on political pressure activity, but on subsequent government policy, is an imperfect basis for a conclusion about group activity, since factors other than industry characteristics also intervene to affect policy. But for what they are worth, these results also fail to offer much support for the free-rider notion. For example, concentration is often insignificant and often has the wrong sign in cross-industry models of US tariffs and changes in tariff levels. Real P. Lavergne, *The Political Economy of U.S. Tariffs: An Empirical Analysis* (Toronto: Academic Press, 1983), table 7.2. William R. Cline finds concentration insignificant in a model of US nontariff protection (*Exports of Manufactures from Developing Countries,* Washington: Brookings Institution, 1984, table 2-6.19).

Standing Political Organization

Naturally, if individuals or firms with a common interest do not form a standing organization to embody that interest, their voices will not be heard as loudly as they might be on a given future occasion. The greater a group's standing organizational capacity for political action on all issues, the greater the opposition that is likely to appear in a given trade protection episode. Even assuming firms have perfect information about their economic interests, we expect a striking difference between the actual political behavior of two firms with equivalent trade interests if one has developed an experienced Washington staff dedicated to coalition-building and lobbying for the firm, and the other has not.

For our purposes, the interesting aspect of this obvious connection is that business associations and government-relations departments may form, grow, and decline for reasons largely independent of international trade. A major change in political organization, however exogenous it may seem, will greatly amplify or diminish the waves of trade politics, if other conditions are present.

Chapter 3 looked back at the last decade and saw the explosion of lobbying capacity as a key element in the rise in anti-protection behavior. Looking toward the future, these enlarged capabilities will not be used on trade issues simply because they exist. But now that all these political law offices and representatives have been established, they will be attempting to generate work on some issue. Unless the organizational expansion is reversed, then even if international market conditions should change, observed political pressure, from both pro- and anti-protection sides, may not decline as much as the economic change would imply. Furthermore, older associations are likely to remain more sensitized to international issues than they have been during most of their history.

Internal Diversity

A group that has overcome the free-rider problem and diffusion of interest, and has provided itself with a standing political organization, may still undertake less anti-protection activity than some trade interests would imply, because of a diversity of interests merged through the organization. The more diverse a standing organization's membership, with respect to the specific trade in question, the less the organization as such is likely to do in opposition to a product-specific protection proposal.

Washington business offices vary from the representative of one firm, to the association speaking for a single, narrow industry, to the broader or "conglomerate" organizations. The Business Roundtable consists of some 200 chief executives of the top industrial, financial, and commercial companies in the country; the National Association of Manufacturers has a membership of some 13,500 industrial enterprises; the Chamber of Commerce of the United States is a vast federation of some 257,000 firms and associations, including manufacturers but also many small service companies and even agricultural employers. Farm organizations range from those devoted to a single commodity, to the multi-commodity National Grange and the huge American Farm Bureau Federation.

Divisions can occur in a small organization as well as a large one. Chapter 3 illustrates differences within various companies and specific industry associations over trade issues. In addition, some narrow standing organizations representing sectors who appear to have strong stakes in trade are structured to include import-competing producers as well. Textile manufacturers are members of the National Cotton Council, the farmers' organization. Prominent companies that own copper mines are members of the copper fabricators' organization. Some consumer organizations include labor unions as members, and the unions' positions on international trade reflect their interests as producers more than as consumers. Chapters 3 and 6 also show that the broadest, conglomerate business associations have avoided taking strong action, or even any action, against most product-specific protection. They may take a clear stand on generic trade legislation, bills that do not identify which specific industries will be affected. But in more specific cases, the greater the diversity of interests, the greater the chance that co-members will resist those seeking to have the organization speak out against protection. The more uniform the interests, the more likely the organization's support will be.

Competing Policy Priorities

Most US political players have multiple political objectives. Manufacturers are deeply affected by tax and regulatory policies, and by government participation in standard-setting for their products. Agricultural groups generally give priority to major farm legislation, particularly in years (like

1981 and 1985) when it is due for renewal. Organizations representing household consumers are understandably concerned with product information, quality, and safety: "truth-in-packaging," or prompt notification of auto owners about car defects.

Even when their trade interests are challenged, groups will be less active on the anti-protection side during periods when other political opportunities or threats involve larger stakes for them, than during other periods. In recent years, agricultural exporters have been diverted away from anti-protection work by the struggle over renewal of general farm legislation in 1985 and by the collapse of land values and commodity prices that made financial survival a live question for some farmers. In the international arena, attention shifted somewhat to new schemes for promoting exports, and opposition to foreign agricultural assistance. These projects may have left less time to work on import protection issues.

CHARGES OF UNFAIRNESS

Given an economic environment and a political structure of potentially active organizations, the strategies and tactics chosen by other players in the game will also diminish or energize the political opposition. For instance, in some episodes the pro-protection side files petitions under US law alleging that imports are unfairly traded. Of course, to do so is to exercise legal rights; such a course may not be undertaken deliberately as a political tactic. But the step necessarily becomes a part of the surrounding political process as well, intentionally or not.

In politics, going to battle on behalf of imports already has a vaguely unpatriotic image, and this is especially so in the case of imports that are attacked as unfair. Thus, because potential anti-protection actors anticipate especially negative reactions from fellow citizens and politicians in such episodes, they will be less vigorous in opposing proposals for protection that highlight charges of dumping, subsidies, or other unfair trade practices.

Charges of unfairness have been especially prominent in steel episodes, where they appear to have dampened anti-protection responses. Across the full sample of different types of groups, a group's opposition seemed significantly lighter or absent in the four episodes where such charges of unfairness were a prominent part of the case (see appendix C).

Particularly at the time of writing in 1986 and early 1987, the general discussion in Washington was marked by frequent statements that other countries were not playing fair in international trade. In the spring of 1987, even the Reagan administration seemed to ratify this view by imposing retaliatory trade sanctions on Japan for the first time since World War II. In this climate, few "free traders" took a stand against the sanctions in general, although no less than 74 organized interests, from the San Diego Sheriff's Department (worried about calculators) to General Electric (concerned about refrigerator parts) lined up to seek exemptions for products in whose import they had an interest. The trend seemed to be almost toward identifying "free traders" with "those who tolerate unfair treatment of Americans." Continuation of the trend would probably continue to have a dampening effect on anti-protection activity.

THREATS OF RETALIATION

Foreign governments sometimes threaten retaliation if the US should increase its barriers. When retaliation threats name specific American sectors as likely victims, or when these sectors have felt such retaliation in the past, they are more likely to express political opposition than otherwise. European Community spokesmen from time to time have mentioned American soybeans as a possible target, and the soybean association worked fairly seriously against the 1984 steel quota proposals. After China slashed US wheat imports in 1983, the wheat growers became the most active US group pressing for a compromise solution to the dispute over textile protection. And the response to the *American* retaliation list for semiconductors from those dependent on Japanese products suggests that a similar response can be expected from import-related interests if their trade flows are specifically threatened.

It is also conceivable that threats of retaliation tend to energize all US exporters who depend on the threatening country, even when the threat is not specific about the victims. But a preliminary econometric test does not discover such a general exporter response to vaguer threats (see appendix C).

PRIVATE AND PUBLIC LEADERSHIP

Finally, this analysis would be incomplete if it failed to recall that leadership, or its absence, shapes political participation. Personal forces in politics tend to resist generalization, let alone quantification, but their influence is undeniable. The stronger the initiative taken by individuals and firms outside government, or by politicians and officials, the stronger the anti-protection response that will appear in a given episode.

If firms had perfect information about how trade policy proposals would affect them, then there would be less scope for the would-be political entrepreneur or leader. If organized groups had no competing political or commercial priorities, they might monitor the trade-policy arena more continuously themselves and have less need to rely on others to sound the alarm. If commercial actors were all experienced in the process of Washington policymaking, they might know just when to take the initiative, what specific benefits to seek, and what they needed to offer in return.[11] It is the holes in such assumptions that create the space in which political leadership makes a difference.

For one thing, active effort will influence how other parties perceive their own interests. In fact, many firms and unions have little direct stake in a given product-specific trade decision, and they devote little effort to measuring their own indirect interests. But often many do have a tie to some directly-affected party, and sometimes to people on both sides. Frequently, many groups' net interests are not clear-cut, and thus their perceptions are more subject to influence than a simple economic interpretation might imply. Political appeals, by themselves, will not move a group from the sidelines into heavy activity, but they can make a more moderate difference. If nothing else, an active partisan may convince a third party to refrain from helping the other side.

This more fluid reality is available to both pro- and anti-protection forces. To take a clear illustration, in the 1950s coal miners and independent oilmen sought an oil import quota, and they touched off a considerable struggle. The coal association was the most vigorous force on either side. The railroads also wanted these quotas, as far as Congress could see. They testified and signed public statements to that effect. As a matter of fact, though, the railroads were in a complicated position: they carried coal, but they also bought coal and oil to burn in their engines, they carried some oil in tank cars, and they had other important customers with overseas interests. The coal lobby had seized the initiative, and railroad executives had simply

---

11. For interesting thoughts on corporate political strategies more generally, see David B. Yoffie and Sigrid Bergenstein, "Creating Political Advantage: The Rise of the Corporate Political Entrepreneur," *California Management Review*, vol. 28, no. 1 (Fall 1985), pp. 124–39.

responded passively to an isolated request for a favor from a customer, without any systematic study at all of how the bill's ramifications would affect their multiple interests. They had little strong feeling for the quota.

One wonders what would have happened if, before the National Coal Association took the initiative, an exporters' association had approached the same railroads to ask them to present testimony for expanded foreign trade. They might conceivably have testified on the opposite side and in doing so have been equally convinced that they were acting rationally for their self-interest. . . But what actually happened was that they were organized by the National Coal Association, and that fact determined the stand they took.[12]

Meanwhile, on the other side of the street, the Washington office of Cleary, Gottlieb, Friendly, and Ball, representing the Venezuelan Chamber of Commerce, had in fact perceived analogous opportunities to mobilize opposition to oil quotas. Starting from the premise that most businessmen would not recognize any self-interest in the matter, they conducted statistical studies identifying which US industries exported to Venezuela, and wrote letters to specific firms warning them that the proposed bill could end a specified dollar amount of their business. In one campaign they appealed to 500 companies to express their opposition to their congressmen, and got aid from 150 of them. Even though the cost of becoming informed might have caused these firms to take a "free ride" in the absence of leadership, they did act. Even the New England textile industry, dependent on fuel oil, flooded Congress with protests, and New England congressmen took the lead in opposing the measure, despite their advocacy of protection on other products.[13]

Our previous chapter discusses more recent examples of such leadership. Some efforts were frustrating experiences for anti-protection activists, but others helped produce broad coalitions representing hundreds of thousands of people.

Not only can private initiative and counterinitiative be crucial; the President and members of Congress themselves can affect the level and direction of this activity to a considerable extent. For example, during the Tokyo Round

---

12. Raymond Bauer, Ithiel de Sola Pool, and Anthony Dexter, *American Business and Public Policy: The Politics of Foreign Trade* (New York, NY: Aldine, 1972), p. 370.

13. Ibid., pp. 376–77; George Ball, *The Past Has Another Pattern: Memoirs* (New York, NY: Norton, 1982), p. 103. Note that the coal industry, when prodded by a Brazilian customer, was an anti-protection actor in steel 1984 (appendix A).

negotiations, the office of the Special Trade Representative (STR) used its international bargaining positions and its network of private-sector advisory committees quite deliberately and actively to mobilize support in particular congressional districts where support was lacking. When the package went to the Congress, STR Robert Strauss hosted a White House breakfast for the major Washington trade lobbyists, urging them not to fight ratification, but rather to help secure it. In recent years, some group representatives have told us the Reagan Administration has put forth less effort of this type. Indeed its positions alarmed some advocates of open trade enough to convince them there was a need to shock the White House into taking trade seriously.[14] If the stimulus had been stronger, the anti-protection response might have been stronger.

Leadership efforts, like entrepreneurship, are difficult to predict or explain, and they are certainly constrained by the conditions considered earlier. But within those constraints, leadership strength and skill will also shape anti-protection activity in the future.

Summary

In conclusion, the extent of future anti-protection activity will depend primarily on two obvious fundamentals: the strength of pro-protection campaigns, and the degree to which the economy and particular sectors depend on the imports and exports affected by those proposals. Particular sectors will then probably manifest more or less political opposition than their simple trade interest would imply, because of a host of secondary considerations, including macroeconomic conditions, the sector's microeconomic characteristics, the degree and form of group organization for political activity, and the tactics used by potential opposition leaders and other players in the game.

But in the end, what role does this interest-group opposition play in US decision making? Is US trade policy any different because of it? This important issue occupies chapter 5.

---

14. On the other hand, during the summer of 1986, after the House of Representatives had passed a major potentially restrictive trade bill, President Reagan invited 135 Washington representatives of export and import interests to the Executive Office Building to hear him personally appeal for their help in fighting such measures. (*Washington Post,* 18 July 1986.)

5 Anti-Protection Activity and US Policy Outcomes

Up to this point, we have described and explained changes and differences in groups' political opposition to US protection. But their efforts must ultimately be considered in relation to the goal of influencing government action, of making US import policy more open or less restrictive than it would otherwise be.

Does anti-protection activity in fact contribute to this goal? Granted that some groups are more active than others, how do politicians and bureaucrats respond to such opposition? Would things have been different if no such opposition had appeared? In short, "so what?" After first concentrating on group political behavior, we now shift to thinking about the government's behavior, although a complete analysis of trade policy formation would be beyond this study's purpose.

This chapter argues that, perhaps contrary to appearances, anti-protection activity does appear to have made a significant difference. It has influenced, in the intended direction, the substance of official decisions on product cases. It has made the political process into something different from the more familiar one. Of course, in most episodes there was *some* increase in trade protection. But adding the anti-protection ingredient helped produce a different omelette—one involving fewer or looser restrictions than probably would have prevailed without it.

Identifying true influence is a notoriously speculative and problematic venture, and we do not claim to have produced definitive answers. Nor is it our position that interest group activity, pro or anti, is typically the dominant—or even the primary—influence over official trade policy decisions. Later in this chapter we will address other important influences: the impact of macroeconomic conditions, and in particular the roles of politicians, policy officials, and government institutions. But in the opening pages of this chapter, we shall remain within a narrower—albeit very important—framework, treating the relationship between anti-protection activity and policy outcomes without regard to other factors and forces.

The chapter begins by assessing the outcomes of product episodes, how much additional protection—if any—resulted in each. Next we show that in episodes in which anti-protection forces manifested greater opposition, the resulting government decisions tended toward greater restraint—rejection of new protection or only slight increases. This is particularly true if one measures activity in relation to the economic size, or *political potential,* of the anti-protection interest most affected. The chapter then explores possible counterarguments, or other influences that might also have accounted for these same results. In so doing, it discusses the political institutions and processes through which such decisions are made in the United States, emphasizing relevant features that are sometimes slighted and which clarify the role of anti-protection activity. It concludes that while a number of these other influences appear significant in their own right, none of them can dissolve the apparent connection between political opposition and policy decisions.

The Variety of Policy Outcomes

Not all pro-protection pressure leads to higher import barriers. And actual increases are not all created equal. New restrictions vary significantly in degree, and these differences in degree are important to parties on all sides.

The headlines by themselves often paint a misleading picture of what governments are actually doing in markets. In many instances, the US government denies requests for protection. This study is designed to represent the variety of reality, including decisions that could be considered "successes" as well as "failures" from the point of view of anti-protection forces, while attempting not to prejudge what accounts for the decisions.

Table 5.1 contrasts these product-specific decisions roughly according to the degree of change in policy by the end of the episode. We emphasize that the focus here is on comparing *changes* in the levels of protection, regardless of what the initial levels were, and not on comparing the levels of protection existing at the conclusions of the episodes. Similarly, the analysis to follow takes the status quo in each episode as a baseline, and asks what produces or inhibits increases in the degree of protection.

In one case, the government removed existing protection—in 1974 when the Congress defeated a bill to renew the Sugar Act and its quota system. In four others, Washington denied proposals for increased protection. In each

TABLE 5.1   US policy decisions in product episodes as measured by change in protection

Reduction of protection	No change	Slight increase	Substantial increase	Sharp increase
Sugar 1974	Sugar 1978–79	Textiles 1983	Footwear 1976–77	Sugar 1981–82
	Autos 1982–83	Textiles 1984	Steel 1977–78	
	Copper 1984	Textiles 1985–86	Autos 1980–81	
	Footwear 1984–85		Steel 1982	
			Steel 1984	

of the other nine cases, it added or tightened import restrictions by varying degrees.

Comparative classification of the import policy changes in the other nine episodes is not easy, since in none of them was the form of new protection a simple tariff increase applied to imports from all sources, as spelled out in appendix D. This table reflects judgments about each increase along two subdimensions:

• *severity,* judged by the apparent effect of the new measures on the share of US consumption supplied by imports from all sources

• *rigidity,* meaning the degree to which the form of new restrictions contributes to their duration, by making them harder to change in the future.

By these criteria, in the 1981–82 sugar case, for example, the government increased protection sharply. Newly imposed quotas covered all foreign suppliers, whose share of US consumption fell by 33 percent between 1981 and 1982–83. And in this episode, severity was joined by rigidity. This protection was an integral part of the statutory program for maintaining prices for domestic sugar producers, and hence it was difficult (though technically not impossible) to alter without changing the law.

The footwear decision of 1977, by contrast, added substantial protection, but was not as great a change in either of these two senses. Washington exempted many suppliers; newly controlled imports (from Korea and Taiwan) were 54 percent of the global total by volume and 31 percent by value. During the period of restraints, the Korean and Taiwanese share of the US shoe market fell by some 17 percent, comparing the actual 1978–81 average with the actual 1976 share. Meanwhile, the market share of imports from all sources combined were held steady in 1977–78 at the pre-restraint level.

Import volume actually declined by about 7 percent. The form was negotiated export restraints for a limited (four-year) period, under authority of section 201 of the Trade Act of 1974, rather than restrictions specifically written into law. Another petition to the US International Trade Commission (USITC) to extend the new protection beyond the deadline was rejected by President Ronald Reagan.

In the 1983 textiles case, the US negotiated a new set of quantitative restrictions affecting exports from China, which supplied 11 percent of the volume of US imports of clothing and textiles. Because of market conditions and the levels and product coverage of these new limits, China's share of the overall US market did not decline but rather increased by 11 percent in the 1983–1984 period, from 1.8 percent to 2.0 percent. The import growth rate was cut in half compared with the three-year period prior to restraints, but this still permitted annual growth of 20 percent per year. Imports from all sources combined expanded their market share by 21 percent after this new China agreement took effect. Rigidity in this case was intermediate between the other two examples. The form was negotiated export restraints, but this action was somewhat more difficult to reverse than in the case of shoes, because the textile restrictions were imposed outside the framework of section 201 and could be renewed more easily. In sum, this action is rated as a slight increase in restrictions.

As explained at the outset, these cases are neither a strictly representative sample nor a universe of all episodes. Thus, any conclusions based on them are not definitive. They do encompass, however, most of the major product-specific trade battles over the past decade. And as argued in chapter 2, any bias in the selection probably works against the view that anti-protection political activity makes a difference.

The Impact of Anti-Protection Activity

The episodes that resulted in greater increases in protection tend to feature lesser effort by opposition forces. Conversely, the greater the anti-protection activity, the more restrained the policy change tends to be. This relationship can be seen first, in a simple cross-tabulation of the two variables—activity and policy outcomes—and secondly, and more strongly, in a refined version.

How do we measure activity? As discussed in chapter 3, and spelled out in appendix A, we rate the known activity of each group in each episode as to the extent of effort and risk undertaken. If we assume that such actions

TABLE 5.2   **Aggregate activity ratings**

Heavy	Moderate	Light
Autos 1982–83 (337)	Footwear 1976–77 (129)	Steel 1982 (61)
Steel 1984 (335)	Textiles 1984 (126)	Textiles 1983 (52)
Textiles 1985–86 (280)	Autos 1980–81 (117)	Sugar 1981–82 (48)
Footwear 1984–85 (182)	Copper 1984 (103)	Steel 1977–78 (33)
	Sugar 1978–79 (72)	Sugar 1974 (19)

are politically cumulative, then we can regard the summed activity scores for an episode as an approximate indicator of aggregate overt opposition to protection in that episode. An episode's total score would be increased both by the participation of more groups at relatively low levels of effort, and by much more intense effort by a few groups. While we have assigned these scores carefully according to explicit rules, they reflect judgments and undoubtedly some omissions, and so we do not wish to place much weight on small differences. Still, major variations across episodes are obvious in table 5.2. After each episode is shown its aggregate activity score. These ratings include steps taken by both national and international actors.

Table 5.3 then shows the relation between this activity and the policy changes that resulted from each episode. If this small set of cases were a sufficient basis for conclusions, it would suggest that greater anti-protection

TABLE 5.3   **Anti-protection activity and policy outcome**

Aggregate activity	Policy action				
	Reduced protection	No change in protection	Slight increase	Substantial increase	Sharp increase
Heavy		Autos 1982–83 Footwear 1984–85 (50%)	Textiles 1985–86 (25%)	Steel 1984 (25%)	
Moderate		Copper 1984 Sugar 1978–79 (40%)	Textiles 1984 (20%)	Autos 1980–81 Footwear 1976–77 (40%)	
Light	Sugar 1974 (20%)		Textiles 1983 (20%)	Steel 1977–78 Steel 1982 (40%)	Sugar 1981–82 (20%)

effort is associated with somewhat greater success, from the anti-protection standpoint. If success had been defined as no increase in protection, then increasing the effort from "light" to "heavy" raised the odds from .20 to .50. If, instead, success were defined as avoiding a substantial or sharp increase in protection, then light opposition is associated with a 60 percent chance of failure while heavy activity is associated with 75 percent chance of success.

A summary measure of association between two ordinal variables is given by the statistic $lambda_{sp}$. This statistic varies between 0 and 1, and is interpreted as the probable improvement in prediction. A $lambda_{sp}$ of .50 means that knowing the independent variable will increase the number of correct predictions of the dependent variable by 50 percent, compared with predictions based on knowing only the relative frequencies of different policy decisions. For table 5.3 the value of $lambda_{sp}$ is .20. Of course, given the small number of observations, a change in one or two could have a substantial effect.[1]

The correlation in this table is positive but weak. Moreover, practitioners' recollections of certain episodes raise an important question about whether it is aggregate activity, measured in this way, that influences policy. For instance, in the 1984 steel case quite a number of steel users testified before Congress and the USITC against protection, though selectively in some cases, and their appearances are reflected in the relatively high aggregate score. Yet trade policy practitioners, interviewed in 1985 with that episode relatively fresh in their minds, recalled things rather differently: steel users were "just not organized," "many of them were scared to death" and "didn't come in." On the other hand, many interviewees recalled the copper fabricators as a rare and perhaps unique example of a user group that was active and effective in the anti-protection cause in 1984. Yet aggregate activity, as we have measured it, was less in the copper case than in 1984 steel.

These perceptions may suggest that what mattered to public officials with influence over these decisions was not so much the absolute level of anti-protection activity, as the share of the total affected community it was seen

---

1. The formula for $lambda_{sp}$ is: $(\Sigma f_i - F_d)/F_d$, where f_i is the largest frequency for each class of the independent variable, and F_d is the largest marginal value of the dependent variable. This statistic is used because it is asymmetric, in the sense that it makes use of the information that one variable is intended as the cause and the other the effect, and because it has an operational interpretation. G. D. Garson, *Handbook of Political Science Methods* (Boston: Holbrook Press, Inc., 1971).

as representing. Participants may have had a stronger impression of the copper users because a larger *proportion* of them mobilized than in steel, where the potential coalition is far bigger, and the turnout—while larger in absolute terms than for copper—was smaller in relation to that potential. This possibility suggests a more refined variant of the activity variable, one which is, in fact related to policy decisions much more strongly.

ACTIVITY RELATIVE TO POTENTIAL

This variant assumes that government decisionmakers are sensitive to the different sizes of constituencies that would pay a cost from protection for a particular industry, such as steel or sugar, and that they respond not to the absolute amount of political opposition, but to activity relative to the potential they expect. The larger a group is, the more money it can commit, the more "troops" it can conceivably deploy through letter-writing and other activities. Politicians, in this view, infer that costs and opposition are less serious if only a small fraction of the potential appears on their scene, even if this activity is large in comparison with some episode involving a different industry. Thus, significantly more activity will be required in a steel case than in a copper case in order to have the same effect.

It may also be assumed that US leaders respond primarily to domestic petitioners and are not so affected by international interests' efforts.[2] This second variant, then, maintains that the greater the *domestic* opposition, relative to the potential in that case, the more policy makers will resist new barriers. Since the ultimate political weapon is the vote, probably the best single indicator of domestic political potential is the total number of employees working in the sector or belonging to an organization. We assume conservatively that the potential coalition is limited to groups likely to be affected most immediately. With consumer products, we include only the retailers and dealers whose profits or jobs may depend on sales of imports.[3] For

---

2. This assumption may be misleading to the extent that international activity takes the form of publicizing the costs of protection to Americans, or other steps that might shift official thinking indirectly, rather than "pressure" in the usual sense, or to the extent that it alerts officials to the foreign relations implications of trade-restrictive action.

3. This assumption may involve some exaggeration in the actual stake of retailers, but it also omits entirely the millions of Americans employed in other sectors that would pay a price for protection, such as shippers, port communities, and banks, not to mention final consumers.

TABLE 5.4   **Ratings for aggregate activity relative to potential**

Heavy	Moderate	Light
Sugar 1978–79 (3.97)	Footwear 1976–77 (0.78)	Textiles 1983 (0.06)
Sugar 1981–82 (2.68)	Footwear 1984–85 (0.58)	Steel 1976–77 (0.05)
Sugar 1974 (1.31)	Textiles 1985–86 (0.51)	Steel 1982 (0.05)
Copper 1984 (1.10)	Steel 1984 (0.49)	
Autos 1982–83 (1.03)	Autos 1980–81 (0.20)	
	Textiles 1984 (0.18)	

industrial inputs, the coalition includes only producer sectors that are highly dependent on the traded good. For copper and steel, only sectors for which the input accounts for 25 percent or more of the value of output are included. For sugar, the threshold is 10 percent.

Let us also assume that politicians will make a further adjustment in the case of import users or distributors to reflect the lower relative intensity of their interest. While copper imports loom large to copper miners, copper is but one of a number of inputs to the copper-using firm. Thus our politician might assume that the user firm would be unlikely to mobilize its political resources to the same extent in order to influence copper import policy. Employment figures on the anti-protection side are therefore reduced, by multiplying each sector's actual employment by the sector's input coefficient for the traded good. Thus, the smaller the share that copper contributes to a copper user industry's output, the more the adjustment reduces the employment figure. For retailers, we multiply employment by the value share of imports in domestic consumption of the product concerned. The final estimate of political potential of the opponents in an episode is the sum of these adjusted employment figures.

We then divide each episode's aggregate activity rating for domestic groups by its adjusted employment figure. Table 5.4 shows the ranking of *relative* activity which results.[4]

---

4. It is not obvious whether exporters are or are not perceived as part of the potential domestic political force in opposition to proposals for product-specific protection. A new measure might hurt them only indirectly, in which case politicians might assume that they are not part of the potential coalition. But if it stimulated retaliation, it could impose a much more direct cost on them. Exporters have acted in some episodes. However, exporters are excluded because interviews suggest that at least some political leaders assume exporters are not directly affected by US protection, and because most actual domestic activity was not by exporters.

TABLE 5.5   **Domestic anti-protection activity, relative to potential and trade policy**

Relative activity	Policy action				
	Reduced protection	*No change in protection*	*Slight increase*	*Substantial increase*	*Sharp increase*
Heavy (1.0+)	Sugar 1974 (20%)	Autos 1982–83 Sugar 1978–79 Copper 1984 (60%)			Sugar 1981–82 (20%)
Moderate (0.16–0.99)		Footwear 1984–85 (17%)	Textiles 1984 Textiles 1985–86 (33%)	Steel 1984 Autos 1980–81 Footwear 1976–77 (50%)	
Light (0–0.15)			Textiles 1983 (33%)	Steel 1977–78 Steel 1982 (67%)	

Table 5.5 then arrays relative activity against the outcomes of these episodes. It shows a rather strong and consistent positive relationship. The US government does tend to behave as this variant would lead one to expect. The value of $lambda_{sp}$ is .60.[5]

ACTIVITY AND TYPE OF WORKER REPRESENTED

Another possible relationship, suggested by several whom we interviewed, is based on the premise that what matters is not just the magnitude of activity,

---

5. An attempt at multivariate analysis of policy decisions has not proved useful, for several reasons. We have only 14 observations, and are working with fairly rough indicators for the independent variables. The episodes were chosen to explore anti-protection activity across a range of products and policy outcomes, but not for purposes of testing a broad array of hypotheses about other determinants of US trade policy. In any case, the logit technique employed in chapter 4 and explained in appendix C finds that none of the variables discussed in this chapter seems to be significantly related to these policy decisions. Of course, with a small number of cases, conclusions are highly sensitive to a change in one or two episodes. For instance, when the two extreme outcomes (1974 sugar and 1981–82 sugar) are excluded, the logit estimates confirm the impression from table 5.5 that relative domestic anti-protection activity has a significant negative effect on import restrictions. No other variable appears significant in that reduced sample.

but its source. This suggests that the American political process systematically favors certain groups over others, reflecting, presumably, the way that Americans view different types of economic activity. Public opinion since the birth of the republic has looked upon farmers as the bedrock of national prosperity, a sentiment that has long outlasted the movement of our vast majority off the land. Industrial producers command lesser but considerable respect: they are *making* something. Service positions are, as a class, viewed with less respect, even by many who hold them. And last on the respect ranking might be those whose service occupation involved the marketing of foreign products (for example, importers, Toyota salesmen).

Politicians and interest groups express and reflect such values repeatedly. The agricultural community seems to many to be the most appealing anti-protection force (the only one "without negatives," as one former senior trade official put it).[6] The copper users gained credibility in 1984 by linking their case to American production jobs, and Caterpillar's efforts on steel that same year were noted and respected. Conversely, more than a few politicians dismiss retailers as "just out to make a buck," suggesting that service enterprises—unlike factories—serve no broader purpose for society.

Let us therefore examine the case outcomes in relation to the type of US workers represented by the lead groups on the anti-protection side.

Table 5.6 shows a consistent positive association between type of job represented and policy outcome; the *lambda* value is .60.[7] There are anomalies: farmers won only a limited.victory in textiles 1983, and service workers and marketers of foreign products did better in autos 1982–83 and footwear 1984–85 than this factor would lead one to expect. Still, on balance, these episodes lend credence to this idea.

Does this affect our basic argument: that activity influences policy? On balance, we conclude that the argument still stands. There is, across our 14 cases, a clear positive association between activity relative to potential and

---

6. Because the interests of exporters (including farmers) are typically less direct than those of users or retailers, we excluded them from our estimates of potential domestic anti-protection forces above. However, when farmers *do act*, as in the 1983 textile episode, they would be expected—according to this view—to receive a relatively more sympathetic hearing than other categories of workers.

7. The use of four rather than three labor type categories raises the apparent correlation, because of the way the *lambda* statistic is calculated. If the farmer and industrial labor cases were merged, the *lambda* value would drop to .40. This suggests that the relationship to outcomes, for our episodes, is weaker than that for activity relative to potential.

TABLE 5.6   **Type of anti-protection labor and trade policy**

Type of labor involved	Policy action				
	Reduced protection	No change in protection	Slight increase	Substantial increase	Sharp increase
Farmers			Textiles 1983 (100%)		
Industrial labor	Sugar 1974 (20%)	Copper 1984 Sugar 1978–79 (40%)		Steel 1984 (20%)	Sugar 1981–82 (20%)
Service workers		Footwear 1984–85 (25%)	Textiles 1984 Textiles 1985–86 (50%)	Footwear 1976–77 (25%)	
"Foreign" product marketers		Autos 1982–83 (25%)		Steel 1977–78 Autos 1980–81 Steel 1982 (75%)	

Note: Classifications here reflect the authors' judgment of which US-based groups were most active and were perceived by practitioners as playing the lead role in the anti-protection coalition.

type of labor represented: the occupation variable distributes the episodes in a manner that is very close to the previous table, which measures not "what you do" commercially but "how much you do" politically. It is possible, therefore, that some of the correlation between activity and outcome is in fact attributable to the type of occupation represented. It is at least as likely, however, that certain occupational groups tend to mobilize proportionately more than others, and that it is actually the mobilized activity to which the government is sensitive. Our data are insufficient to settle the matter. A reasonable conclusion is that both of these variables are relevant to government trade decisions, with relative activity apparently the stronger of the two.

OPPONENTS RELATIVE TO PROPONENTS

This study concentrates on the opposition, but it could be, instead or in addition, that the decisions raising barriers relatively more are those in which the proponents mounted larger political campaigns, either absolutely or relative to their own potential. It would also be interesting to have the ratio of pressures actually manifested by the two sides, in order to see whether protection failed to increase in some episodes because pro-protection pressure was weaker, relative to the opposition, than in the other episodes. Unfortunately our resources do not permit us to replicate this investigation on the other side of the battle (though later research might do so).[8]

A ratio of the coalitions' underlying power resources is more feasible. The corresponding hypothesis might be that the greater the proponents' power resources relative to those of the opponents, the more politicians will increase protection, and the stronger the opponents, the less the increase. It turns out, however, that such a proxy measure does not in fact add much to our ability to interpret these variations. This section reports evidence for this point.

As discussed earlier in this chapter, we mean by political potential the resources that private interests could bring to bear to influence a policy decision. We need then to develop ratios of the political potential of the anti- and pro-protection forces in each episode, as indicated by adjusted employment.[9] Let us assume that the pro-protection side is limited to all those employed in producing the products to be protected, those whose jobs are directly threatened by foreign competition. On the anti-protection side, we use the adjusted employment figures for directly affected sectors—users in the case of steel, copper and sugar, and retailers in the textile/apparel, automobile, and footwear cases—as described earlier in the chapter.[10]

---

8. Focusing on characteristics of the protected US industry, Vinod K. Aggarwal, Robert O. Keohane, and David B. Yoffie seek to explain "the dynamics of negotiated protectionism" by examining three variables: barriers to entry into that industry, its size, and barriers to exit. Like others who have analyzed the politics of protection, they hold that distress in the industry is a key determinant of *initial* US government decisions to provide trade relief. Their primary purpose differs from ours, however, in that they seek to explain not "why governments impose [specific] trade barriers" but "what happens to negotiated protectionism in the United States *after* agreements have been reached" (emphasis in original). Variables such as these could usefully be included in a future study encompassing both the pro- and anti-protection sides. See their "The Dynamics of Negotiated Protectionism," *American Political Science Review*, vol.81, no.2 (June 1987), pp. 345–66.

9. Previous studies have investigated whether differences in industries' employment size, or their shares of the national or district labor forces, help explain differences in the levels of protection the government provides. See, for example, Real P. Lavergne, *The Political Economy of U.S. Tariffs: An Empirical Analysis* (Toronto: Academic Press, 1983); William R. Cline, *Exports of Manufactures from Developing Countries* (Washington: Brookings Institution, 1984), ch. 2; Robert E. Baldwin, *The Political Economy of U.S. Import Policy* (Cambridge, Mass.: MIT Press, 1985). The present question is different in two senses: it focuses on the ratio of employment in the opposing coalitions, and it asks about changes in protection, rather than industry differences in levels at the same time.

10. For completeness, we performed the calculations a second time adding in export interests.

T A B L E   5.7   **Relative political potential**
(thousand employees)

Case	Anti-protection potential	Pro-protection potential	Anti-protection ratio
Footwear 1984–85	166.1	114.7	1.45
Copper 1984	39.9	29.1	1.37
Steel 1984	433.6	340.8	1.27
Steel 1982	491.0	506.1	0.97
Steel 1977–78	538.6	552.6	0.97
Sugar 1974	14.5	17.3	0.84
Sugar 1981–82[a]	14.6	17.6	0.83
Sugar 1978–79[a]	14.5	17.6	0.82
Footwear 1976–77	82.7	164.2	0.50
Autos 1982–83	250.5	699.3	0.36
Autos 1980–81	265.7	788.8	0.34
Textiles 1985–86[b]	365.4	1,185.3	0.31
Textiles 1984[b]	272.0	1,163.4	0.23
Textiles 1983[b]	243.0	1,161.0	0.21

Source: Appendix B; Bureau of Labor Statistics, *Employment and Earnings,* various issues.
a. Pro-protection potential in this case includes employment in the corn sweetener industry, as well as that in growing cane and beet sugar (as indicated by the number of farms) since growth in that industry has been largely a result of the artificially high price of sugar. The same figure had to be used for both 1978 and 1981 because official data on the number of cane and beet farms is not available for 1978.
b. We limit this ratio to apparel to avoid having to count clothing manufacturing workers on both sides—as users of textile fabric.

The "relative weights" of each side and the ratios between them are presented in table 5.7. (The components from which the table is developed are provided in appendix B.) To take one example, consider the 1984 proposal for steel protection. On the proponents' side, direct employment by steel producers amounted to 340,800 in 1983. On the other side, the

---

To measure exporter political resources, we draw on the exporter tables in appendix B. We include sectors selling to countries that would be affected by the proposed barrier, but only if they ship at least 3 percent of their total production to those countries—a demanding threshold. Total employment in those industries, discounted by the share of total production exported to the target countries, becomes the adjusted employment estimate. Adding exporters to the ratio for each episode, however, changes our results not at all.

TABLE 5.8   **Relative political potential (excluding exporters) and trade policy**

Ratio of anti-protection political potential	Policy action				
	Reduced protection	No change in protection	Slight increase	Substantial increase	Sharp increase
High		Footwear 1984–85 Copper 1984 (67%)		Steel 1984 (33%)	
Medium	Sugar 1974 (17%)	Sugar 1978–79 (17%)		Steel 1982 Steel 1977–78 Footwear 1976–77 (50%)	Sugar 1981–82 (17%)
Low		Autos 1982–83 (20%)	Textiles 1985–86 Textiles 1984 Textiles 1983 (60%)	Autos 1980–81 (20%)	

Note: A high ratio indicated a stronger opposing coalition, relative to proponents, and a low ratio, a potentially weaker opposition.

unadjusted employment total for the most dependent steel-using industries was 1,317,620—more than four times the number of producers. The downward adjustment for intensity reduces this indicator to 433,550, or 1.3 times the number of those engaged in steel production (see tables B.11–B.13).

The relationship between these ratios and policy decisions is then depicted in table 5.8. This small set of cases does not seem to present much of a consistent pattern either way. Proponents of protection seem to have accomplished more when the relative potential of the opposition was medium than when it was either very weak or very strong.

The degree of political unity or division within the pro-protection camp might also be worthy of further investigation. According to some participants, the 1974 defeat of the Sugar Act was due in part to a division in the ranks of the supporting coalition, regardless of organized opposition. The sugar program was amended on the floor of the House in a way that made it more onerous for growers. Some growers decided they no longer needed a sugar program and at the last moment told their congressional supporters to vote against renewal. Later sugar episodes were also marked by internal division to a less decisive degree. Another variable that might usefully be examined is the degree of import penetration or other economic distress in the sector seeking protection.

Except in the measurement of political potential, however, our empirical analysis has been limited to the anti-protection side. Hence, we cannot rule out pro-protection pressure itself, or divisions among proponents, as explanations for the observed variation in policy decisions. However, the political potential ratio does not consistently identify cases in which the government resisted proposals. The type of worker represented by anti-protection forces does appear to matter, but it is a somewhat less reliable predictor—across our cases—than activity relative to potential. Thus far, therefore, the proposition that political effort contributes to anti-protection outcome would appear to be sustained.

But what of other variables that might explain government decisions? Can the variety of outcomes be explained by prevailing macroeconomic conditions? Or might they be the product of features of the larger American political system? We turn now to the relationship of these broader forces to the choices politicians made in our 14 product episodes.

Variations in Macroeconomic Circumstances

Among the many conditions affecting US trade policy, the most prominent—and frequently cited for their impact—are changes in macroeconomic variables. Much has been written, and appropriately, about how protection decisions are affected by unemployment, inflation, or the strong dollar. Across these 14 episodes, however, none of these is very helpful in explaining variations in government action.

Common sense suggests, and some research[11] confirms, that depressions are favorable for protection, and booms make trade liberalization more likely. The effect may be independent of interest group activity. On this argument, political leaders will be more sympathetic to a particular industry request

---

11. Timothy J. McKeown, "Hegemonic Stability Theory and 19th Century Tariff Levels in Europe," *International Organization,* vol. 37 (Winter 1983), pp. 73–92; Giulio M. Gallarotti, "Toward a Business-Cycle Model of Tariffs," *International Organization,* vol. 39 (Winter 1985), pp. 155–88; James Cassing, Timothy McKeown, and Jack Ochs, "The Political Economy of the Tariff Cycle," *American Political Science Review,* vol. 80 (September 1986), pp. 843–62.

TABLE 5.9   **Unemployment and trade policy**

Rate of unemployment	Reduced protection	No change in protection	Slight increase	Substantial increase	Sharp increase
		Policy action			
Low	Sugar 1974				
Medium		Sugar 1978–79 Autos 1982–83 Footwear 1984–85	Textiles 1985–86	Footwear 1976–77 Steel 1977–78 Autos 1980–81 Steel 1982	Sugar 1981–82
High		Copper 1984	Textiles 1983 Textiles 1984	Steel 1984	

when alternative work opportunities are scarcer. In good times, they would expect workers displaced by imports to be more easily absorbed elsewhere in the economy. When inflation is raging, it will concentrate official minds on ways to dampen price increases and will stiffen resistance to protection requests, and vice versa. When the overall trade balance is negative, this will undermine official confidence in the ability of the economy in general to compete effectively, and will lower the government's resistance to such requests, while a positive balance will reinforce confidence. Political leaders everywhere also fear a trade deficit for its effects on social stability and the nation's international economic influence.[12] When we examine recent experience in the light of such macroeconomic conditions, however, the connection is elusive, for different apparent reasons with different variables.

For one thing, these episodes were not selected with a test of such hypotheses in mind. The national unemployment rate, measured in the year

---

12. If one deemphasizes the role of interest groups and assumes a strong state guided by a liberal ideology, such relationships would not necessarily hold. In that case, severe unemployment, low inflation, or a large excess of imports over exports, would not necessarily be expected to cause governments to take some new measure to intervene in markets. Government response would almost certainly depend as well on the perceived cause of the problem, and perceived likely effects of various tools. It might easily take a form other than import barriers. And as Peter Gourevitch, *Politics in Hard Times* (Ithaca, NY: Cornell University Press, 1986) emphasizes, states' responses to depressions vary considerably according to domestic politics. The relation between one's conception of the political process and one's explanation of policy outcomes is addressed later in this chapter.

TABLE 5.10   **Inflation and trade policy**

Rate of wholesale inflation	Policy action				
	Reduced protection	No change in protection	Slight increase	Substantial increase	Sharp increase
High	Sugar 1974	Autos 1982–83		Autos 1980–81 Steel 1982	Sugar 1981–82
Low		Sugar 1978–79 Copper 1984 Footwear 1984–85	Textiles 1983 Textiles 1984 Textiles 1985–86	Footwear 1976–77 Steel 1977–78 Steel 1984	

prior to the episode's final decision, varied only moderately between these episodes, ranging between 7.1 percent and 9.6 percent, with one exception. The exception was 1973, when unemployment was 4.9 percent. The following year, the Sugar Act was defeated, consistent with this hypothesis, but we doubt that the national unemployment rate was a major reason for this sugar decision, as discussed earlier. Otherwise, the relationship was not in the expected direction.

In these episodes inflation rates, as indicated by the producer price index in the year prior to each decision, varied widely, from 1.2 percent to 14.1 percent. But policy restraint was no more likely in high-inflation years than in periods of relative stability, judging from these episodes.

In a larger set of cases, of course, inflation might prove to be more important, and few would doubt that the US trade balance would prove more influential still. These conditions could clearly be expected to alter the policy environment, by stimulating or diminishing pressure for protection from private groups, and by affecting official attitudes directly. And many of these episodes occurred during a period of rapid deterioration of the US trade balance. None of them happened during a trade surplus, and only one when the trade account was close to balance. But in the other cases, imports (measured as c.i.f. dollar value) in the year prior to the decision ranged from 120 percent to 160 percent of exports, a much greater variation than one would find in any comparable postwar period.

We find no significant association between this range of deficits and policy outcomes, however. If anything, Washington rejected slightly more of the reported cases faced in the most recent years of severe trade deficits than in other periods.

TABLE 5.11   **The trade balance and trade policy**

Ratio of imports to exports	Policy action				
	Reduced protection	No change in protection	Slight increase	Substantial increase	Sharp increase
High Ratio (1.4+)		Copper 1984 Footwear 1984–85 (40%)	Textiles 1984 Textiles 1985–86 (40%)	Steel 1984 (20%)	
Lower ratio (1.3−)	Sugar 1974 (11%)	Sugar 1978–79 Autos 1982–83 (22%)	Textiles 1983 (11%)	Autos 1982–83 Footwear 1976–77 Steel 1977–78 Autos 1980–81 Steel 1982 (44%)	Sugar 1981–82 (11%)

It it also reasonable to argue that a change in the dollar's exchange rate will affect trade policy. A rise in the dollar would encourage imports and discourage exports, and thus touch off the same policy effects as a change in the trade balance due to other causes. The late 1960s and the mid-1980s both saw an overvalued dollar and growing pressure for trade protection, despite declining unemployment. But in the present sample of episodes, the results are the same as with the trade deficit. (Only the textile 1983 episode, a slight increase, would shift from the lower to the upper section of table 5.11.)

In sum, macroeconomic hypotheses, somewhat surprisingly, do not help much to account for this pattern of policy outcomes, although few would deny that the general trade politics climate was seriously affected by the dollar and the trade imbalance. This politics is also importantly shaped, however, by broad features of the American political system. We now move to consideration of this system.

The Broader Political Context

Evidence of the links between opposition activity and outcome appears in a fuller and somewhat different light when interest-group struggle is seen in its broader political context—institutional, ideological, and international. This context adds other dimensions that also appear to make some difference in the likelihood of policy change. But on balance, this look at the context adds strength to this chapter's main argument, by providing additional reason to expect that anti-protection activity will make a difference.

AMERICAN POLITICAL INSTITUTIONS

Although it may not seem obvious at first, US political institutions themselves have operated as restraints on increases in protection, across all of these cases. Such a contextual element is not visible within the perspective this chapter has followed to this point—the most common view of trade policy formation in the United States, known to analysts as interest-group pluralism. From this perspective, private groups animated entirely by commercial self-interest are the chief shapers of policy. Groups having conflicting interests clash and struggle with each other, and the strongest wins. Or groups engage in logrolling to form alliances seeking particularized benefits for all, distributed according to the political resources each brings to the alliance. In the purest version, this view pictures the government or state as nothing more than an arena for group struggle and a passive computer of the result, not as an initiator, builder of coalitions, or foreign-policy maker. The classic example of a raw pluralist process is the creation of the Smoot-Hawley Act in 1930.[13] Policy, in short, is seen as a function of the relative weights and pressures of the private groups.

But a comparable study of pro-protection forces would probably have shown that the proponents actually deployed more lobbying and constituent communications than did their opponents in most cases. If policy formation

---

13. Described in E. E. Schattschneider, *Politics, Pressures, and the Tariff* (New York, NY: Prentice-Hall, 1935). Actually Schattschneider himself denied that pressures always must "run wild"; one of his main theses was that governing means managing pressures, rather than simply yielding to them, and that political leaders had managed these very poorly. Elsewhere in political science, though, government has sometimes been likened to a computer, which receives "inputs" from society, and emits "outputs," or policies. Likewise, many economists writing on trade policy have operated within strictly pluralist political assumptions, postulating a domestic "market for protection," in which international relations and national political institutions are virtually invisible, and officials' behavior is seen as trading policies for votes, assuming that they are motivated only to maximize their personal self-interest in reelection. Some of the more recent works in this genre are beginning to incorporate more international and institutional ideas. For example, see Robert Baldwin, *The Political Economy of U.S. Import Policy.*

had been simply a group tug-of-war, pro-protection campaigns would probably have won every time, even if not to the same degree.

An alternative analytical perspective maintains that the state or government dominates its society and its foreign economic policy, not the other way around. The initiative comes from inside, not from outside. The government imposes a structure on society and specifies the decision-making process— the timing of decisions, who participates, and what the agenda is. Established political institutions determine what policy instruments are even available at any one point in time.

In this alternative view, the highest interest of any state is security, and concerns about security, alliances, and diplomacy often color foreign economic policy, especially during periods of high tension and war. During calmer intervals, states still need alliances, and import protection will always seem to be a disturbance to be avoided if possible, if it would disturb allies and friends abroad. Past commitments to international regimes like the General Agreement on Tariffs and Trade (GATT) are also embedded institutionally and persist, for some of the same reasons that domestic institutions do so. International relations are a major part of the context that shapes governments' trade policies.[14]

While the second view can be exaggerated, we have each tried to show elsewhere that the first alone is inadequate; a combination of the two is best.[15] American institutions make executives and legislators the strongest potential players in the game of mutual influence between public and private actors, and give them a position from which to take initiatives. Political leaders sometimes directly encourage private groups to enter the political

---

14. State-centered conceptions and institutions are currently enjoying a boom of renewed interest among some social scientists. See Peter J. Katzenstein, ed., *Between Power and Plenty* (Madison: University of Wisconsin Press, 1977); Stephen D. Krasner, *Defending the National Interest* (Princeton, NJ: Princeton University Press, 1978); James G. March and Johan P. Olsen, "The New Institutionalism: Organizational Factors in Political Life," *American Political Science Review*, vol. 78 (September 1984), pp. 734–49; Peter Evans, et al., eds., *Bringing the State Back In* (Cambridge: Cambridge University Press, 1985); Judith Goldstein, "The Political Economy of Trade: Institutions of Protection," *American Political Science Review*, vol. 80 (March 1986), 161–84; and G. John Ikenberry, David A. Lake, and Michael Mastanduno, eds., *The State and American Foreign Economic Policy*, a forthcoming special issue of *International Organization*.

15. John S. Odell, *U.S. International Monetary Policy: Markets, Power, and Ideas as Sources of Change* (Princeton, NJ: Princeton University Press, 1982); I.M. Destler, *American Trade Politics: System Under Stress* (Washington and New York, NY: Institute for International Economics and Twentieth Century Fund, 1986), esp. ch. 5.

process to support their initiatives, including trade liberalization, or to oppose others, including protection. Group activities do not always signify private interests taking the initiative. When groups opposed President Woodrow Wilson's proposal for substantial tariff reduction in 1913, he took to the stump to rally popular sentiment for progressive reform against the special interests, and public pressure helped secure passage of the bill. When President Jimmy Carter sought ratification of the Tokyo Round agreements in 1979, his Trade Representative, Robert Strauss, invited group represen- tatives to the White House to ask them to lobby on behalf of the final bill. More recently in 1985, Senator Bob Packwood (R-Ore.), who was then chairman of the Finance Committee, was firmly opposed to the Jenkins textile bill, and he reportedly urged the port and retail interests of the northwestern United States to speak out against the bill.[16]

One landmark study of trade policy formation in the 1950s concluded, in fact, that business groups were often ambivalent or inactive, and that the true initiators in policy campaigns were typically legislators and bureaucrats, with interest groups playing the role of support troops, furnishing information and political services. It found that business leaders too, when thinking about protection, are influenced by their attitudes about US foreign policy (inter- nationalists versus isolationists), not only by "what they make." Group activities can even be echoes of government leaders, playing a role because politicians and bureaucrats encourage them to do so.[17]

To be sure, US institutions are distinctive globally in the degree of access they give to private groups, and the constraints they place on official authority. Members of Congress are especially vulnerable to such group pressures from their districts, much more so than executive officials. So the first perspective contributes insights that are important, especially for understanding congres- sional behavior, and most especially during periods when the executive takes a passive political stance toward pressures. It is also true that in the last decade, the United States has modified its trade policy machinery in ways that make it less difficult to add protection through administrative means.

However, US political institutions are also distinctive in the degree to which they divide authority, between the executive, legislative, and judicial branches, and within the branches. Thus, the same machinery that gives

16. Interview.
17. Raymond A. Bauer, Ithiel de Sola Pool and Lewis Anthony Dexter, *American Business and Public Policy: The Politics of Foreign Trade* (New York, NY: Aldine, 1972).

private groups much access to the policy-making process also creates, among other things, a status quo bias. Any proposal to change a basic policy must clear numerous hurdles. The institutions provide many opportunities for the status quo to ambush a bill as it crawls through one or more House of Representatives subcommittees, to full committees, to the floor, and on through the Senate. A more centralized set of institutions might be easier to capture, at least in one sense. And in this period of history, the one seeking an exception or change in basic policy is the pro-protection advocate. One reason for this is a second important contextual element in postwar American trade politics: liberal ideology.

IDEOLOGY

A second, basic force that has tended to restrain increases in protection in all these cases, and which also may be masked by recent events, is the distinctively strong influence in America of the general belief that markets, whether domestic or international, should manage themselves, unless a convincing case for an exception can be made. The idea of comparative advantage is fairly widely understood, especially among the most influential political leaders, and especially by comparison with earlier periods of US history. Of course the liberal ideology was modified significantly in the 1930s and 1940s by adding a public commitment to maintaining full employment and stabilizing the national economy, and certain other exceptions are widely supported. But regarding trade, the 1930 Smoot-Hawley precedent is universally associated with disastrous consequences, leaving a strong aversion to "protectionism," at least at the level of general policy preferences. We believe few US political leaders today are privately eager to impose import restrictions in general, and that many prefer privately to avoid using this particular tool.[18]

It is true that recent discussions of reciprocity and foreign industrial policies do indicate growing support at least for contingent bargaining protection, i.e., threats of import restrictions, to be carried out only if a foreign government refuses to make a concession to the United States. This support

---

18. Among those placing particular emphasis on this factor is Judith Goldstein. See "A Reexamination of American Trade Policy: An Inquiry Into the Causes of Protectionism" (Ph.D. dissertation, University of California at Los Angeles, 1983).

is probably a genuine change. And some leaders certainly make public, rhetorical statements that are quite inconsistent with the principles of comparative advantage. But in contrast to other countries, few elected American politicians have actually advocated general use of import barriers as a desirable national development strategy for the United States.

Because they have shared, for the most part, this broad ideology, presidents—and to a lesser extent congressional leaders—have used their institutional resources to initiate trade liberalization in the period since World War II. Official actors have varied and multiple goals: not only winning greater personal influence or reelection, but also advancing the welfare and security of their agencies, their districts, their country, and their allies abroad. Presidential initiatives have for years been intended to help build a domestic exporter constituency for trade liberalization. The prospect of the reward of increased exports has encouraged exporters to speak out for trade liberalization, and has helped members of Congress to resist and manage pressures. When leaders have given legislators a chance to vote for other political alternatives to protection, such as adjustment assistance to import-affected petitioners, they have further strengthened the political rationale for legislators to resist import restrictions.

Thus, to return to the apparent association between anti-protection effort and policy decisions, if the typical US leader begins with a personal liberal tilt, then in a given case, less than an overwhelming demonstration of political opposition is sufficient to stiffen his or her resistance to a proposal for additional intervention in import markets. Even if the "anti" forces outside government are smaller or less well-mobilized than the proponents, the presence of visible opposition may reassure the many politicians whose convictions run to open trade, and most of whose own constituents are not deeply concerned about the imports in question. Public evidence that protection would hurt other citizens gives liberal-leaning leaders political support they feel they need in order to do what they actually feel they ought to do: to deny or water down the request.[19] The greater the opposition, the more likely they are to deny it altogether. Presumably, if a general pro-protection ideology

---

19. Of course some politicians and officials are exceptions. For a fuller argument and evidence, see Destler, *American Trade Politics,* esp. ch. 5. This is a key reason why we feel it is useful to study anti-protection activity in its own right, without having comparable evidence on the pro-protection campaigns, although ideally—as explained in chapter 1—one would like to study both side by side.

dominated, a less than overwhelming demand for protection would be sufficient to tip the decision in favor of protection.

THE INTERNATIONAL SYSTEM

A third general influence that changed relatively little during the 1975–85 decade was the nature of the international system. If major shifts had occurred in the distribution of power among nations, or in international cooperative arrangements like the GATT, trade policies of the United States and other states might have shifted with them.[20] But those conditions did not vary in a pattern that can account for recent US trade decisions.

These episodes did involve different target countries, and an international interpretation might expect that the United States will be more restrained in raising trade barriers against stronger states, or those that are its more important allies, and less restrained against others. But this idea, too, fails to add much to these particular cases; there is very little tendency in this direction. If anything, here the United States seems slightly more likely to hit big allied countries harder than small ones. Of course, our closest allies are also our largest trading partners and thus present, in the main, the strongest trade threats. Four of the most substantial increases concerned steel and autos, affecting Europe and Japan especially, while only the 1977 shoe case and the 1982 sugar case seriously affected small states.[21]

Similarly, an international focus might expect that proposals that breach or threaten US international obligations or the GATT will fare less well than others, regardless of domestic political opposition. In our episodes, this proposition finds some support, although only two of the 14 proposals were involved. The 1982–83 domestic content bill and the 1985–86 textile bill would have unquestionably violated international obligations. Neither of

---

20. For recent expositions of such arguments, see Stephen D. Krasner, ed., *International Regimes* (Ithaca, NY: Cornell University Press, 1983 and 1985); Robert O. Keohane, *After Hegemony: Cooperation and Discord in the World Political Economy* (Princeton, NJ: Princeton University Press, 1984); and David A. Lake, *Modern Mercantilism: International Economic Structures and American Trade Strategy, 1887–1939* (Ithaca, NY: Cornell University Press, forthcoming).

21. Again, we are comparing changes, not levels, of protection. The average US tariff on manufactured goods imported from developing countries exceeds that affecting more developed states.

these bills was adopted, although the government had previously given the auto industry a substantial increase in protection by means of a negotiated export restraint, and it provided, in 1983–86, several slight increases in protection for textiles. Four other initiatives that did not involve such breaches of GATT were defeated as well.[22]

Most important, however, has been the impact of international relations in constraining executive branch protection decisions more generally. If we conceive of the President and trade subordinates as officials with some degree of autonomy, a liberal-trade ideology, and a responsiveness to international obligations, they will be aiming, in many cases, to deny or limit trade protection. The existence of visible lobbying by anti-protection forces can make it easier for them to do so.

What other factors might reinforce—or dilute—such an anti-protection official tilt? One factor that could surely strengthen it would be the existence of policy alternatives to restricting trade. One factor that would limit it would be presidential political commitments to particular industries.

THE EXISTENCE OF POLICY ALTERNATIVES

If a President has other trade policy options—ongoing trade-liberalizing negotiations, or the presence of a substantial trade adjustment assistance program—he could well be less likely to opt for protection. Confronted with a specific hardship case, it is often difficult for a political leader to do nothing. If he can offer something else to a trade-impacted industry—adjustment aid, for example—or if he can argue that protection for that industry will undercut a major, ongoing trade expansion initiative, he may be more likely to deny or limit import relief.

---

22. A clear application of this particular hypothesis would require resolving several ambiguities. Most important, many proposals fall into what is called the ''gray area''—quantitative restrictions that contravene the GATT Article XI prohibition, but which are widely used in the form of negotiated export restraints, and which GATT members partly legitimated in the textile sector with the subsequent Multi-Fiber Arrangement. More generally, the increased use of VRAs can be explained by the fact that they allow officials to circumvent both the GATT process abroad and the legislative process at home. See C. Fred Bergsten, Kimberly Ann Elliott, Jeffrey J. Schott, and Wendy E. Takacs, *Auction Quotas and United States Trade Policy*, POLICY ANALYSES IN INTERNATIONAL ECONOMICS 19 (Washington: Institute for International Economics, September 1987).

Our episodes do not offer a very good test of these propositions, since only the first four chronologically happened when either option was available. As a set, their outcomes were not noticeably different from those of the other cases. However, if one looks within specific episodes, the presence of trade adjustment aid as an alternative appears to have made some difference. President Jimmy Carter offered it to auto workers in 1980 while resisting protection; President Gerald R. Ford did the same for footwear makers four years earlier. In each case, however, the President's successor opted for substantial protection one year later.

PRIOR POLITICAL COMMITMENTS

Next, we reach the obvious and important question of commitments originating with government leaders. As a part of some electoral campaigns for the presidency, a candidate may make a promise to an industry to increase its protection. If so, then the subsequent decision-making process will almost certainly be—and appear to be—"pre-wired," or tilted away from the normal status quo, regardless of how much opposition to the increase is displayed. Candidates John F. Kennedy and Richard M. Nixon, for example, made such promises to the textile sector in 1960 and 1968, respectively. Even then, however, the degree of change is usually subject to some influence.

During the 1980 campaign, both the auto and textile industries extracted general pledges from candidate Ronald Reagan. On autos, Reagan promised to "try to convince the Japanese" to limit their exports. On textiles, he agreed that imports should grow "in relation to" growth in the domestic market. Both of these commitments could be expected to make a difference in White House handling of specific protection initiatives, and probably did make it especially difficult for opponents to prevent any increase in those sectors. All three subsequent textiles cases in this study ended in slight increases, and the 1980–1981 auto episode yielded a substantial expansion in protection implemented by Japan.

Another form of precommitment came in sugar 1981–82, when the administration accepted legislation leading to protection in order to win support for its 1981 budget package. While that legislation did not guarantee sugar quotas, it made them highly likely because the statutory alternative was direct budget payments to support sugar prices.

It is impossible to judge the general importance of such commitments from the evidence of only one President, especially their importance relative to

TABLE 5.12 **Prior political commitment and trade policy**

Prior commitment?	Policy action				
	Reduced protection	No change in protection	Slight increase	Substantial increase	Sharp increase
Yes			Textiles 1983 Textiles 1984 Textiles 1985–86	Autos 1980–81	Sugar 1981–82
No	Sugar 1974	Sugar 1978–79 Autos 1982–83 Copper 1984 Footwear 1984–85		Steel 1977–78 Footwear 1976–77 Steel 1982 Steel 1984	

other influences. But a simple cross-tabulation (table 5.12), similar to the earlier ones, does suggest a positive relationship. Aside from the special case of sugar, however, these commitments resulted, on the average, in relatively modest increases in protection.

But so far as one can tell from a single President's behavior, this factor may help at least to explain differences between no change and slight change. Once a President has made such a political commitment, even a heavy mobilization by an "anti" coalition might not be sufficient to put a case in the extreme-left column. And it does account for the largest anomaly, the episode where substantial activity relative to potential did not lead to a less restrictive result.

The 1981–1982 sugar case was the one that departed most from the outcome that would be expected from relative anti-protection activity. Opponents expended one of the heaviest efforts relative to their size, and yet the government imposed a more severe increase of protection than in any other case. This result was due largely to log-rolling over a contemporaneous nontrade issue, which injected a major one-time bias against even the most vigorous sugar user or consumer effort. The Reagan Administration was on record as opposing creation of a new sugar price support program. But during the summer of 1981 Reagan's team had been laboring hard to secure congressional support for his first budget proposal, particularly among Republican and conservative Democratic members. Some of them held back their votes until the last moment, when their price was withdrawal of the President's opposition to renewing the sugar program. David Stockman, Reagan's Director of the Budget and chief operative on that issue, agreed to trade sugar, along with other things, for the budget, which then passed.[23] During the subsequent battle over sugar itself, the administration's opposition was difficult to detect. Even though the House of Representatives defeated the sugar bill, proponents got it included in the final farm law during the House-Senate conference. A plunge in sugar prices in early 1982 triggered the quotas in May.

ONE EPISODE AFFECTS ANOTHER

Similarly and finally, it is helpful to note also that the occurrence or outcome of some episodes is sometimes influenced by previous or contemporaneous protection battles, even if this factor may not loom large relative to others. For instance, some Washington talk in 1984 predicted that if the President was going to yield to pressure from the steel industry for a substantial increase in its protection, he would feel compelled to say "no" to some other industry in order to remove the smudge on his credentials and reaffirm his calls for internationalist and free-market policies worldwide. The copper decision was contemporaneous, and the President rejected the appeal. But we suspect the answer in that case would have been the same if no steel case had been pending: the copper fabricators employed more workers than the mines; there was no effective protection option other than an "OPEC" for copper.

More important, it is argued that by arranging for substantial new protection for the automobile industry in 1981, through Japanese export restraints that were extended several times, for example, the President probably helped defeat the subsequent proposal for legislated protection. A similar executive "down-payment" might also have helped keep steel and textile protection from increasing more, or more rigidly, than they did. (By the same token, the fact that auto workers mounted a major campaign for the more ambitious domestic content bill, even though it failed, might have prevented export restraints from ending sooner than they would have without that huge fight.)

Finally, a denial of protection—such as President Reagan's footwear decision in 1985—may be cited in support of proposals in Congress aimed at making such protection more likely in the future. Even as this study is

---

23. See David Stockman, *The Triumph of Politics: The Inside Story of the Reagan Revolution* (New York, NY: Harper and Row, 1986), ch. 8. John Breaux (D-La.), a leader among sugar congressmen, clarified that he had only been "rented, not bought."

being completed, the United States Senate has in fact acted favorably on such a proposal.

But such executive moves may also produce an unintended political-economic effect in the opposite direction. The above argument takes pro-protection pressure as given, and reasons that given such pressure, Congress will add protection if the President does not. But increasing barriers around a sector such as steel probably slows the movement of people and resources out of that sector, slowing or preventing a decline in political pressure that would be likely otherwise, at least over the longer run. So piecemeal "downpayments" may also make subsequent protection struggles more likely and longer lasting than would be the case without a policy change. On balance, the net direction of these two effects probably depends on the initial political power of the import-competing industry: the weaker it is, the more likely it will adjust rather than securing more protection.

Conclusions

If anti-protection activity has increased, what difference does it make? Many things influence a state's trade policies, and we have not attempted a full analysis of US import policy here. What has been largely overlooked in previous research is the possible effect of domestic political opposition to protection. The 14 cases analyzed here suggest that greater opposition is associated with rejection of new barriers or lesser increases, and that when opposition effort is weaker, protection increases more. At least in a liberal-leaning government or state that needs international alliance solidarity, such opposition can make decisions to reject or resist protection more likely, regardless of the activity of the proponents.

While correlation does not prove causation, several attempts to reveal this association to be spurious have failed. We have mentioned several influences—particularly macroeconomic—that we believe to be important in general, but which are unable to explain differences among these decisions made in the recent era. Two other things do seem to differentiate among these episodes to a significant extent: the type of worker represented by the lead anti-protection force, and whether or not the President had made a prior promise to increase an industry's protection.

It is possible that economic conditions in the petitioning industry, such as import penetration or unemployment, or the degree of political pressure it actually brings to bear, will also be significant additions, and might partly supplant the apparent anti-protection effect. We have not been able to examine these possibilities in detail. We do know that the potential power ratio of the proponent and opponent coalitions does not help much to explain variation among our episodes. This chapter has also shown that neither the international power of the target country, nor the prevailing national unemployment or inflation rates, nor the overall trade balance can account for the observed differences among decisions. Moreover, the selection of cases probably imparts, if anything, a bias against the notion that anti-protection activity matters.

In the absence of more convincing evidence to the contrary, we therefore conclude that the anti-protection phenomenon has made a difference, in the intended direction. Observers and analysts of trade policy need to give more attention to this phenomenon.

6 Generic Trade Issues: A Different Pattern

If the reader has stayed with us to this point, he or she may be afflicted with a nagging concern. We have highlighted in this book a considerable *rise* in political resistance to product-specific trade protection. Yet the dominant trade-political trend of the 1980s, most authorities believe, has been in the opposite direction. Beginning in 1985 and continuing to the present, Congress has seized the initiative and pressed forward with broad legislation likely, if enacted, to increase American trade protection. Participants and observers of this drama regularly point to the *demise* of the old coalition in support of liberal trade. As one representative critique put it in May 1987,

Virtually no one is clamoring for free trade, despite the obvious benefits to exporters and consumers. Constituencies that ought to be fighting protectionism have simply given up or vanished. Big business, for example, used to be solidly in favor of free trade, but now business is divided between firms and industries that want foreign markets and those that fear foreign competition. American agriculture used to be a powerful free trade constituency. Today, however, many farmers are disillusioned with the world market as the answer to their problems, in part because they face competition from other countries whose agriculture is becoming more productive.[1]

Taken by itself, such a characterization seems a bit overstated. For one thing, the "free trade" lobby was never as strong, or as self-starting, as the above words imply. For another, there has developed, in 1987, a significant, business-based lobbying effort to modify the most restrictive provisions of the pending legislation. Nonetheless, there seems to be broad agreement among trade policy specialists that, at least in struggles over legislation, the balance of forces has shifted in the restrictive direction. At a May 1987 Washington conference sponsored by the National Bureau of Economic

---

1. William Schneider, "Talking Free Trade but Acting Protectionist," *National Journal*, 2 May 1987, p. 1082.

Research, Congressional Research Service specialists Raymond Ahearn and Alfred Reifman summarized the national politics of current legislation as: "Decline of free trade coalition. Defections from business and agriculture while labor aggressively backs Gephardt amendment."

Do such characterizations of trade politics contradict our finding of increased anti-protection activity as documented in previous chapters? We think not. The key distinction lies in the nature of the trade policy issues involved.

In contrast to the *product-specific* struggles analyzed in the bulk of this study, the 1987 legislation deals primarily with *generic* trade policy issues, resolutions of which apply, in principle, to all products. Among the matters at stake are proposed changes in the administrative protection statutes: sections 201 (escape clause) or 301 (dealing with "unreasonable" or "unjustifiable" foreign trade practices), or the rules governing remedies for imports alleged to be subsidized or dumped. At issue is what criteria should control the decisions on specific cases, who should make the decisions, under what procedural constraints (including time limits), and so on. The very description of these laws can make eyes glaze over. But their outcomes, reflected in the wordings of technical trade statutes, contribute importantly to overall US trade policy, to how open the American economy is to imports.

This study does not treat such generic trade policymaking in the detail with which it addresses product-specific episodes. The most important reason, methodologically, is that one cannot treat struggles over generic issues as independent trade policy "episodes" with discrete time periods and relatively independent outcomes, since policy changes come intertwined in omnibus trade legislation. Product cases can be considered as separate events, without undue violence to the real world. Generic cases cannot because outcomes are interdependent: nontariff barrier negotiating authority *and* easing of escape clause criteria in 1974; toughening section 301 and extending GSP a decade later. In the end, Congress typically lumps its decisions together in omnibus trade legislation. And bargaining is intertwined, with the more protection-tilting provisions of such laws often serving as quids pro quo for the liberal ones.[2]

---

2. This suggests that one might better treat as cases or episodes the broad bills themselves: Burke-Hartke or the 1970 "Mills bill" that failed; the 1974, 1979 and 1984 acts; the proposals of 1985 and 1986. But this approach brings at least as many problems. For example, anti-protection (and pro-protection) groups do not typically weigh in on the bills taken as wholes, but on particular provisions that interest them the most: natural resource subsidies, antidumping law reform, etc. Generally, it is easier to rate the outcomes of particular titles on a liberal-restrictive scale than to rate entire omnibus acts.

Our research on recent struggles over generic issues has therefore been less structured and systematic than our treatment of product questions. But it offers, on balance, evidence to support the widespread perception that the "free trade" coalition has weakened. It offers reason to suspect that, even as "special interests" have increasingly asserted themselves on product issues when trade barriers threaten their market position and profits, opposition to new generic trade protection has eroded. There has not necessarily been an abandonment of open trade as a goal. But there has been, among its longtime supporters, rising dissatisfaction with the current US trade situation, which has made them both less resistant to traditional protectionism and more sympathetic to aggressive negotiating tactics over export markets, including threats of imposing new US trade restrictions in retaliation for those encountered abroad. These changes may not be permanent, but they have clearly inhibited anti-protection activity in recent years.

Interviews conducted for this study with veteran trade practitioners, while focused primarily on product episodes, elicited frequent comments as to the weakness or decline, in the mid-1980s of backing for liberal trade policies more generally. In particular, spokesmen for organizations within the anti-protection camp talked of increased strains within their coalitions as specific firms—or subdivisions within firms—found themselves harmed by imports or frustrated on the export side. When we asked one of them whether he perceived an increase in anti-protection activity in recent years, he replied, "No, a diminution." He found it harder to generate counteraction than it used to be; if he picked up the phone it was more difficult to get constituent firms to respond than it was 10 years ago. He found the farm groups, which were once their primary allies, much harder to engage as well.

The impression gained from interviews is reinforced when one examines the stances taken by such broad coalition organizations. If one compares, for example, their testimony at the House Ways and Means Committee trade hearings in 1973 and 1986, it is clear that in the latter year they were less resonantly anti-protection, and more supportive of aggressive export bargaining. In the earlier hearings, for example, the Emergency Committee for American Trade (ECAT) was at least as liberal, on major points, as the Nixon administration: resisting proposals likely to increase protection, championing internationalist approaches.[3] Thirteen years later, its position would

---

3. US Congress, House Committee on Ways and Means, 93rd Cong., 1st Sess., *Trade Reform,* Hearings, 9 May–15 June 1973, 15 parts, Washington, pp. 658–701.

more accurately be summarized as midway between the administration and its pro-protection and unilateralist critics: ECAT backed, for example, some reduction of administration flexibility to deny protection under section 201, and mandatory retaliation—in limited instances—under section 301.[4] There was similar movement between 1973 and 1986 in the stances taken by the National Association of Manufacturers (NAM) and the Chamber of Commerce of the United States.[5]

When one looks at these hearings in general, moreover, there appears to have been a modest drop-off in the proportion of organizations opposing trade restrictions. In 1973, when no fewer than 175 groups presented live testimony in 24 days of hearings, at least 68 of them—39 percent—took strong anti-protection, trade-expansive stances.[6] In 1986, when 78 groups appeared over 8 days, only 27—35 percent—were on the liberal side.[7] If one subtracted from both totals the major coalition organizations—like the Emergency Committee for American Trade and the National Association of Manufacturers—the gap increases: 32 percent in 1973 versus 26 percent 13 years later.

The circumstances were not, of course, entirely parallel. The hearings took place under different ground rules, in different trade-political environments, with witness lists screened by different Ways and Means staff aides. Another important difference was that the executive branch initiated the legislation of 1973 but resisted that of 1986; thus, there was, presumably, less administration activity aimed at lining up supportive testimony. On the

---

4. ECAT also stated that "U.S. trade policy is not the root cause of our foreign trade deficits," and declared as its purpose "to support legislative and other measures that will expand international trade and to oppose those measures that through violations of U.S. international commitments would restrict international commerce." See US Congress, House Committee on Ways and Means, Subcommittee on Trade, 99th Cong., 2nd Sess., *Trade Reform Legislation,* 1986, pp. 183–98.

5. See *Trade Reform,* 1973, pp. 1911–2012 and 1373–1409, and *Trade Reform Legislation,* 1986, pp. 43–111 and 215–35.

6. The stances of the groups that testified were determined through examination of their testimony or the position summaries published by the committee in Part 15 of the hearings. Those who took generally pro-expansion and anti-protection positions were included among the 68.

7. Stances of specific groups were determined through examination of their testimony. This was the first time since 1973 that interest groups could anticipate congressional mark-up of a general trade bill: the 1979 Act was considered under "fast-track" procedures barring committee or floor amendments, and the 1984 Act was pulled together hastily, in the final two months of the 98th Congress.

other hand, the fact that the 1986 House bill was widely labeled "protectionist" might have been expected to trigger greater response from groups fearing adverse effects: in product episodes, the threat of protection has been a primary condition triggering activism to counter it.

Taken alone, therefore, these percentages are merely suggestive. But taken together with our interview evidence and the shifts in the stands of groups that remained anti-protection, they suggest at minimum no increase in opposition to generic trade-restrictive proposals, and perhaps a significant decline.

What might explain a trend so different from the increase in anti-protection activity on product-specific issues? To this question we now turn. First we spell out in greater detail some of the characteristics that distinguish generic trade issues, and their politics, from product-specific ones. Then we move to examination of several forces that appear to have dampened opposition to generic trade protection in the 1980s.

The Nature of Generic Trade Issues

The primary focus of this study has been struggles over product-specific trade decisions. But American trade policy is also the outcome, in important part, of *generic* decisions: to enter a new round of trade negotiations, for example, or to change the definition of "dumping" in our trade remedy law.

Generic issues differ from product issues in several crucial respects:

• their *substance*, which involves not the raising or lowering of a specific import barrier but broader laws affecting such barriers generally

• their *arena for decision*, which is typically not the executive but the legislative branch through its consideration of omnibus trade legislation

• their *pattern of interest group involvement*, which typically features (on the anti-protection side at least) less activity by single-product firms and product groups and more by broad-based umbrella organizations (and, to some degree, multinational corporations).

THE SUBSTANCE OF GENERIC ISSUES

In the 1970s and 1980s, the major general trade issues have been the following:

● *negotiating authority to reduce trade barriers* (proposed 1986–87 and, marginally, 1970; adopted 1974 and 1979)

● *amendments to the "escape clause" (now section 201) governing relief from "fair" foreign competition* (proposed 1970 and 1986–87; adopted 1974)

● *amendments to the countervailing duty and antidumping statutes* (proposed 1984 and 1986–87; adopted 1974 and 1979 and, marginally, 1984)

● *enactment and changes* in section 301, which authorizes action against "unreasonable" and "unjustifiable" foreign trade barriers (proposed 1986 and 1987; adopted 1974, 1979, and 1984)

● *granting and extension of trade preferences* (adopted 1974, 1984)

● *proposals for comprehensive trade restrictions,* for example, the Burke-Hartke bill (see below) and a general import surcharge (proposed 1970, 1971, 1985–86)

● *proposals for general trade restrictions against specific countries, or types of countries,* such as the "Gephardt amendment," which passed the House in 1987

● *proposals for trade reorganization* (proposed 1983, 1987; adopted 1979).

Action under any one of these categories either affects the level of US trade barriers or makes it easier or harder for firms to secure trade relief.

THE LEGISLATIVE ARENA

A second distinguishing feature of generic issues is that they are typically fought out through the legislative process. There are exceptions—the interpretation of a trade law can change,[8] or an administration's general policy posture can shift, as in the Reagan administration's move toward more aggressive use of section 301 and other trade law authorities in September 1985. But in general it is amendments to statutes that change the rules governing trade policy.

---

8. This occurred in the recent Canadian lumber case. See Paul Wonnacott, *The United States and Canada: The Quest for Free Trade,* POLICY ANALYSES IN INTERNATIONAL ECONOMICS 16 (Washington: Institute for International Economics, March 1987), pp. 96–97.

Since the Kennedy Round, there have been seven proposals one can characterize as "major" in terms of their impact on trade politics or trade law, or both. These include one that never got past the bill stage, three comprehensive trade laws that were enacted, two that passed the House of Representatives but not the Senate, and a seventh currently under consideration:

- The "Mills bill" of 1970 would have imposed statutory quotas on textile and shoe imports, and established a mechanism (the "Byrnes basket") for triggering protection for other products.

- The proposed Foreign Trade and Investment Act of 1971 (better known as Burke-Hartke) would have instituted a system of quotas covering the major imported products and would have limited outgoing foreign investment.

- The Trade Act of 1974 authorized US entry into the Tokyo Round, amended the trade remedy laws governing "fair" and "unfair" imports, extended trade preferences to developing countries, and granted (under certain conditions) most-favored nation (MFN) treatment to nonmarket economy countries.

- The Trade Agreements Act of 1979, whose purpose and effect was to implement the Tokyo Round agreements, also rewrote US trade law concerning countervailing duties and antidumping and forced the Carter administration to reorganize certain trade policy functions.

- The Trade and Tariff Act of 1984 renewed trade preferences, authorized negotiation of free trade agreements with Israel and other nations, provided for enforcement of negotiated steel trade restraints, and made modest changes in trade remedy laws (including section 301 governing "unjustifiable and unreasonable" foreign trade practices).

- The proposed, House-passed Omnibus Trade Act of 1986 would have authorized multilateral negotiations, made it easier for industries to qualify for protection under US trade remedy laws, and imposed penalty tariffs on nations running large global and bilateral trade surpluses (among other things).

- Similar omnibus trade legislation is making its way through the legislative process as this study is completed.

Each of these measures, whether enacted or just proposed, contained numerous changes in trade law—some of which acted to increase trade, others to impede it. During the legislative process, policy bargaining took place both within and across issues. In the end, however, each legislator had to vote for or against the resulting package. And if it reached his desk, the President had to make a comparable—albeit more consequential—decision.

PATTERNS OF GROUP ACTIVITY

Concerning anti-protection political activity, generic issues can be distinguished from product issues by the type of group typically engaged. Narrow interests centered on specific products appear to be less active—though not entirely inactive—and general coalition organizations more so.

Narrow *pro-protection* interests have played an important—and perhaps increasing—role. The tendency, judging from recent experience, has been for them to initiate proposals for seemingly "technical" changes in trade laws with generic language actually designed to achieve greater import relief for themselves.

• The steel industry was very active in the rewriting of trade remedy laws in 1979, and after it succeeded in winning substantial changes, it was by far the prime user of these laws in the half-decade thereafter.

• Shoe producers were the intended beneficiary of seemingly technical changes in the criteria for determining injury under the escape clause (section 201), put forward by Senator John C. Danforth (R-Mo.) in 1984; this responded to the finding by the US International Tariff Commission (USITC) earlier that year (based on healthy industry profits) that shoemakers had not suffered injury from the rise in imports.

• "A small group of domestic ammonia [nitrogen fertilizer] producers" was behind the 1983–84 proposal to extend the countervailing duty law to "natural resource" subsidies generally available to an exporting nation's industries; in this case, "opposition . . . crystallized from chemical, agricultural, oil, and other exporting industries," and the provision was not adopted at that time.[9]

---

9. Judith Hippler Bello and Alan F. Holmer, "Subsidies and Natural Resources: Congress Rejects a Lateral Attack on the Specificity Test," *George Washington Journal of International Law and Economics,* vol. 18, no. 2 (1984), pp. 323–28. See also testimony of Richard R. Rivers on behalf of Domestic Nitrogen Producers Ad Hoc Committee in US Congress, House Committee on Ways and Means, Subcommittee on Trade, *Options to Improve the Trade Remedy Laws,* Hearings, March–May 1983, vol. II, Washington, pp. 1076–1119. Occidental Petroleum and Cargill lobbied successfully against this proposal.

• Semiconductor producers, Motorola in particular, took the lead in arguing that "industrial targeting" should be added to the foreign trade practices for which US firms could seek statutory remedies.

Moreover, in instances where a proposal that is generic in form becomes widely perceived as industry-specific in practice, like the natural resource subsidy proposal, it tends to generate the same sort of special-interest anti-protection resistance characteristic of product episodes.

In general, however, narrow interests that gain from trade face a substantial "collective goods" disincentive on generic proposals—their political activity will bring benefits to a broad range of actors, and hence it is likely to cost any particular interest more, at the margin, than the specific gains it can anticipate from success.[10] Those taking the initiative may be able to limit this disincentive by crafting proposals in ways that maximize their likely utility—obviously, the above interests saw trade law "reform" as a means to fight foreign competition. But unless a proposal is likely to strike disproportionately at a particular group gaining from trade, the collective goods problem will inhibit anti-protection reaction from narrowly based groups. And since such groups were primarily responsible for the rise in opposition to product-specific protection, their lesser involvement helps explain the lack of a comparable trend on generic issues.

For broad coalition organizations, the balance of incentives is reversed. The more specific sectors an organization spans, the more likely it will be immobilized by product-specific import issues. Members seeking the organization's support will face more comembers having different interests, provoking them to resist. Thus, because of internal stalemates, broader commercial associations will tend to keep quiet, or to limit their anti-protection steps to letter-writing, on issues of this type—even those that do

---

10. Douglas Nelson argues in a recent paper that effective political pressure felt by Congress on trade remains skewed, as before Smoot-Hawley, in the protectionist direction. But since the Reciprocal Trade Agreements Act of 1934 and successor laws moved Congress out of the business of direct tariff-setting, this has forced import-affected interests to seek relief indirectly—and less efficiently—through amendment of the administrative trade statutes. This has meant, he argues, that US trade statutes have evolved less rapidly—owing to the "collective goods" problem—than did the pre-1934 regime of congressional tariff-setting, but nonetheless in the (same) protectionist direction, reflecting the political imbalance. See Nelson, "The Domestic Political Preconditions of US Trade Policy: Liberal Structure and Protectionist Dynamics" (paper prepared for the World Bank Conference on Political Economy: Theory and Policy Implications, Washington, 17–19 June 1987).

take an open stand in favor of nonspecific, trade-liberalizing laws. The Chamber of Commerce has had a policy of staying out of product-specific issues; ECAT lobbies selectively on those that threaten serious protectionism, like the domestic content and Jenkins bills, but has abstained from others, including "administrative cases" like steel in 1984, even though some steel-using ECAT members see themselves as paying the cost of the steel quotas.

On generic legislative proposals, however, coalition organizations do not face this problem to the same degree. On these, the sharing by member firms of a broad policy orientation—toward expansion of trade—can be sufficient to allow their leaders and staffs the leeway to lobby actively. An example from the 1980s was the successful campaign by ECAT and the Business Roundtable to modify the aggressive reciprocity legislation originally proposed by Danforth, Chairman of the Senate Trade Subcommittee, in 1982. In the campaign against Burke-Hartke, and in favor of what became the Trade Act of 1974, ECAT was a very important influence. President Richard M. Nixon, according to one well-placed source, would not even have sent the legislation to Congress had he not been assured of that group's strong support. And since it was an active lobbying organization with a trade focus, a strong staff, and a blue-ribbon corporate membership, ECAT was a force to be reckoned with.

The constituencies of such organizations do not always, of course, give priority to trade policy. For the multinational firms that comprise ECAT, the most important federal policy arena is clearly tax legislation—it is that which affects their "bottom lines" in a clear and unambiguous manner. (On the wall in the office of ECAT's executive director is a framed "picture" composed of two sets of numbers: 45–44, and below that 43–31. These represented key Senate *tax* votes in the early 1970s on treatment of foreign earnings.) And one reason ECAT was particularly active in 1970–74 was the threat posed by capital control provisions of the Burke-Hartke bill to the operations of multinational firms.

Trade policy, like exchange rates, affects ECAT members also, but less directly and decisively than tax changes. And firms can respond economically to changes in exchange rates or the level of protection: by producing more outside US borders, for example. Thus, in an atmosphere in which many interests with more direct trade stakes—interests that lack this economic flexibility—are increasing their trade-political investments, it is hard for the coalition groups to increase theirs enough not to fall behind in their relative political influence.

As the case of the Nixon trade proposal suggests, such organizations are frequently urged by executive branch leaders to enter the trade policy fray. ECAT was in fact *created* at the behest of President Lyndon B. Johnson in 1967; Johnson was alarmed about rising protectionism in the wake of the Kennedy Round and felt the need for a political counterforce. More generally, generic trade bills have traditionally been considered at the initiative of presidents seeking renewal or expansion of negotiating authority. These presidents and their aides have needed to nurture coalitions to help enact these bills, and their aides have encouraged their formation. Indeed, at least two experienced Washington veterans interviewed for this study insisted that "There never was a free trade lobby," in the sense of a coherent, organized force that *initiated* pressure for trade policy liberalization. Rather, "People were invited in and organized by successive administrations."

Yet our interviews also elicited a strong consensus that such groups have in recent years become more divided and less effective, and that this is reflected in the current debate. As one long-time backer of open trade put it, "You don't have a broad-based community supporting open trade the way you did in the Kennedy Round."

Why might this be the case? We have already discussed, in prior chapters, forces contributing to the rise of anti-protection activity—the growth of trade, the increase in the number of restrictive proposals, the explosion of lobbying generally. These factors have certainly stimulated activity by coalition organizations as well as narrower interests. But several factors have also worked in the opposite direction and have tended to dampen anti-protection activity on generic issues.

One of them is suggested by the above comment about the need for administration leaders to "organize" the liberal trade forces. In sharp contrast to the legislation of 1962 and 1974, the generic proposals of 1986 and 1987 were initiated not by the President or his trade representative, but by trade activists on Capitol Hill. This could help explain the 1973–1986 difference spelled out earlier in this chapter. In the earlier instance, there was an administration bill, and senior trade officials aggressively rounded up support. In 1986, there was no administration bill and little evidence of executive branch hustling. Moreover, former officials such as William Pearce, Deputy Special Trade Representative in 1972–73, argue that it typically takes a major liberalizing proposal to bring out groups in support. If there is a limited bill, or a "bad bill," which the groups expect the President to veto, their reaction may be to stay out.

A *second* key factor has surely been changes in the trade experience—and hence in the trade policy views—of the groups on which the coalition organizations are based.[11] In the mid-1980s, the US balance of trade turned sharply negative, particularly for producers of agricultural and manufactured goods. Leaders of farm and factory inevitably saw more trade pain, and less trade gain. With a lag, their policy positions reflected this.

Representatives and close observers of these groups regularly spoke, in our interviews, of greater strains within their memberships, caused by more divergent trade experiences. More felt they could empathize with the textile industry! One factor was generational change: the postwar business leaders tended to be globalists and free-traders whose World War II experience made them perceive a strong connection between open markets and world peace. They have gradually been replaced by pragmatists and financiers with more recent historical experience.

But more important, by all accounts, were changes in what trade meant for the bottom line. Due to recent farm trade experience, "You have emerging," said one expert, "a sense that free trade may not be in agriculture's best interest after all." Representatives of groups like the National Electrical Manufacturers Association (NEMA), long backers of liberal trade proposals, began arguing in the mid-1980s that the current situation was intolerable, and that either "real free trade" or "trade war" would be an improvement.

This comment reflects a *third* apparent major reason for weak opposition to generic protection and advocacy of aggressive bargaining; the growing perception, across pretty much the entire community of US traded-goods producers, that the United States has been asymmetrically the victim of unfair foreign trade practices. Increasingly, producer interests have seen the US market as open and others as closed. When firms submitted unfair trade cases, they sympathized. As one veteran coalition leader put it, "Guys like myself used to say, 'Don't believe this fair trade stuff, it is just language used by protectionists.' Now I find myself using it, agreeing with them!"

---

11. The common assumption that a firm's trade positions are "influenced by both the competitive pressure it faces from imports and by the benefits it would receive from easier access to foreign markets" has been verified statistically in a recent study of the 1970s. See Thomas A. Pugel and Ingo Walter, "U.S. Corporate Interests and the Political Economy of Trade Policy," *Review of Economics and Statistics,* vol. 67 (August 1985), pp. 465–73.

In reference to a point made earlier, Pugel and Walter conclude (p. 470) that "the threat to multinational operations apparently was the overriding factor in determining corporate positions on Burke-Hartke."

A related point was made by another veteran of battles against proposed trade restrictions. As has been true for product episodes, the success of those seeking import relief in exploiting the "unfair trade" statutes for generic policy change has moved the struggle to a terrain unfavorable to their adversaries: the "blurring of the distinction between the fair and unfair trade procedures has scared people off from joining the anti-protection coalition." To oppose "protectionism" is still to take the high political ground in the United States. It is another thing entirely to be put in a position of defending "unfair foreign trade practices."

This reason is linked, in turn, to specific frustration with Japan. Said one balanced and sophisticated coalition member, "The Japan thing is serious in undermining the anti-protection coalition. The Japanese are particularly protectionist." Or to quote another, "I drive a German car, and couldn't get away with driving a Japanese car."

Within the broad coalition of anti-protection groups, there are reportedly tensions between organizations representing US producers, like ECAT and the Business Roundtable, and those tied more to import-related or foreign interests, like the newly formed Pro Trade Group. With the blurring of the fair trade-unfair trade distinction in law and policy, tough generic legislation may often be seen as appropriately anti-Japan or anti-Asian, with longstanding "free traders" in the United States quite willing to threaten foreign competitors with its enactment. They may also want to threaten the administration, if they see the executive branch as wimpish, unwilling—as Senator Danforth has frequently put it—ever to retaliate against anybody on anything. Sentiment like this meant a striking lack of voices opposing the spring 1987 semiconductor sanctions against Japan on general trade policy grounds, though many specific interests argued against targeting products in which they had a specific stake.[12]

A final, perhaps less significant explanation for the problems of coalition organizations on generic issues is changes in political Washington, specifically the fragmentation of power on Capitol Hill and the related proliferation of industry representatives on K Street. The former makes it harder for business leaders accustomed to exercising power through their connections with a few

---

12. Witness List, US Department of Commerce, "Section 301 Committee Public Hearings on Possible U.S. Actions in Response to the Apparent Failure by the Government of Japan to Fulfill Its Obligations under the U.S.-Japan Semiconductor Arrangement," 13–14 April, 1987, Washington; processed.

key individuals in the Senate or House leadership; the latter undermines the informational advantages—and hence the credibility—of the staffs of coalition organizations. The more that member companies have their own expertise and activist presence in Washington, the more their CEOs are likely to take their cues from their own on-the-ground staffs rather than those of the umbrella organizations. As one businessman put it, "When you have a diverse membership and the membership understands Washington, it's difficult to keep them together."[13]

Conclusions

We would not wish to stretch our evidence on generic trade policymaking too far. We did not conduct the same sort of comparative analysis of generic trade policy episodes that we have carried out for product-specific ones. And even as we write these chapters, Congress is writing what may become new chapters of our national trade law. The political game of 1987 is not over. Anti-protection lobbying is a part of that game; it may yet grow to a point where it contradicts, or suggests important modifications in, the picture painted here.

Nor is the trend discussed here necessarily irreversible. In a period when the US trade balance was turning sharply negative, we would expect to see particular strains in organizations composed of US-based producers, be they industrial or agricultural. But now America's global trade deficit, measured in dollars, has peaked; measured in volumes of goods traded, it has significantly declined. As the dollar-denominated trade imbalance diminishes—as assuredly it will—the political balance should shift back also. The perception of an America uniquely the victim of trade unfairness will probably diminish. And future administration leaders may well be more aggressive and adroit in their trade leadership. It would be risky to assume, therefore, that the apparent erosion of generic anti-protection activity reported in this chapter represents a long-term, irreversible trend, since most of its apparent causes could soon be operating in the opposite direction.

Those caveats aside, however, the apparent weakening of opposition to generically restrictive trade legislation is not inconsistent with the product-

---

13. John Albertine, quoted in Alan Murray, "Conflicting Signals: Lobbyists for Business are Deeply Divided, Reducing Their Clout," *Wall Street Journal*, 25 March 1987.

specific story told in chapters 2 through 5. A generic proposal generates different politics, almost by definition. There is no reason why the rise of limited, "selfish" interests on both the protection and anti-protection side, those directly affected by proposed import restrictions and active in defending their specific interests in the political arena, cannot have coincided with the erosion of the familiar coalition that has supported past import liberalization. And it is certainly consistent with the spreading out of power over public policy which has been the feature of American politics in the last three decades.

What lessons does this experience, together with that which we examined in greater detail in product episodes, offer to public and private trade policy practitioners? We respond to this question in our final chapter, where we summarize our findings and present our recommendations.

7 Findings and Recommendations

The United States government has been under enormous pressure to impose import restrictions in recent years. This pressure has, in turn, generated counteractivity by some of the special interests that benefit from trade and pay the costs of protection. This study has analyzed such anti-protection activity: its sources, its impact, its limits. We have looked primarily at 14 recent episodes where producers of specific products sought trade restrictions, asking which interests were threatened, which ones acted, and what were the results. Our *findings* are summarized here, and spelled out in the core of this study.

Encouraged by such anti-protection forces, US officials have rejected or diluted a number of restrictive proposals. But the net trend, here and abroad, has been toward greater protection. Hence, after we present our basic findings, we seek to draw from them some *recommendations* for those in the United States and other countries who seek to reverse this trend, to find alternatives to the recent global increase in trade restrictions.

Findings

Anti-protection activity has increased, and anti-protection activity has mattered. Those are the two main findings from our analysis of recent trade policy episodes.

Our first conclusion, and perhaps our most surprising one for many readers, is that *there has been a significant rise in aggregate political opposition to product-specific trade protection,* at least over the decade that we studied in detail. From the mid-1970s through the mid-1980s, there was a clear increase in efforts by trade-dependent groups to block or limit new import restrictions. This opposition was mostly reactive and episodic. It came in response to much increased pressure *for* import restrictions. It was still not as great as might have been expected on economic grounds, and it certainly did not defeat all—or even most—protection campaigns. Nevertheless, in cases where such campaigns sought new barriers for imports of automobiles, or copper, or footwear, or steel, or sugar, or textiles, the anti-protection phenomenon grew substantially.

There does not appear to have been a comparable increase in opposition to generic trade-restrictive proposals, such as amendments to trade remedy laws aimed at increasing their utility to firms seeking trade relief. There are in fact indications that, even as resistance to product protectionism was growing, resistance to generic trade protection was eroding.

Leading the opposition to new product-specific trade restrictions were not groups with broad interest in open trade—like consumers or broad commercial organizations—but special-interest groups and coalitions thereof. Among those expanding their political effort were highly dependent exporters, import-using industries, retailers (when a consumer good was at issue), and governments and companies of targeted exporting countries. During the same decade, some former US supporters of open trade policies also became less predictable, or began to favor more aggressive measures against other countries' trade practices. With a few exceptions, multinational companies, banks, and broad commercial organizations avoided involvement in product-specific protection battles, although organizations like the Emergency Committee for American Trade (ECAT) and the Business Roundtable took the lead in resisting proposals by protection-seekers to amend generic trade laws.

Our data suggest that within the overall increase in opposition there was a shift in relative effort among anti-protection interests. Between the early and mid-1980s, activity by import-related groups rose sharply, whereas activity by export-related ones was flat. This was, very likely, a reflection of the rise of the dollar and the surge in the trade deficit during this period, which meant that import users and retailers were depending more on foreign trade, and exporters relatively less so.

The general rise in activity reflected an increase in the standing capacity of groups to mobilize on behalf of trade. Washington representation of business interests was growing during this period; so was sensitivity to the impact of trade policy. Within this environment, *two primary conditions* appear to shape the magnitude of political effort.

First of all, *the greater the dependence on trade*—on the part of the specific group or groups affected—the greater the cost of protection, and hence *the greater the political opposition*, other things being equal. A long-term, structural increase in the internationalization of the US economy underlies the overall rise in anti-protectionism. And a difference between two sectors' dependence on the product or country to be restricted will produce different degrees of political effort.

Second, *the greater the threat to that trade interest,* in the form of pro-protection political campaigns, *the greater the opposing activity.* The last decade has been a period of much more widespread campaigns for protection, affecting more and larger industries. When the political challenge is less serious, opposition forces will likely not make as serious an effort.

Given these two primary conditions, several other factors appear directly or indirectly to increase or diminish the level of anti-protection effort by specific groups:

● *A strong dollar and certain other macroeconomic conditions* increase the pro-protection pressure, and hence will induce greater activity. In addition, these conditions may directly affect commercial interests of anti-protection groups.

● *The greater the import penetration faced by an import-using industry in its final product markets,* the more it will attempt to reduce its costs, and hence the harder it will work politically against protection for its inputs. This stimulant is weaker than it would otherwise be, however, when users decide to seek protection for themselves, and therefore withhold their opposition to protection for other Americans, in order to avoid alienating possible political supporters.

● *Groups having an organized staff for political action already in place* are much more likely to weigh in than the less well organized. An explosion of such standing capacity over the last 15 years has contributed importantly to activity against trade restrictions.

● *The more diverse an organization,* the less likely it is to take a position on a product-specific case.

● *If proponents of protection succeed in labeling imports "unfair,"* this tactic will reduce political opposition, relative to what it otherwise would have been.

● *If another government threatens to retaliate,* this tactic will increase opposition by US exporters, at least on the part of any sector named as a target for retaliation.

- *The greater the effort by executive branch (or private-sector) leaders to stimulate such anti-protection activity,* the greater the activity.

Our second key finding is that *anti-protection political activity matters.* Perhaps contrary to appearances, the growing anti-protection phenomenon does seem to have made a significant difference in product cases, in the intended direction. Political opposition in itself may not have been the most important influence on government action. But it did make the political process into something different from the more familiar one. In episodes in which the opposing forces mobilized greater activity, the trade policy decision tended toward rejection of protection or lesser increases. The type of worker represented by the anti-protection interest made some apparent difference also: those representing farmers and industrial workers did better, on the average, than service interests or marketers of foreign products. But *the best correlation with policy outcome comes from the magnitude of anti-protection activity in proportion to the potential (economic size) of the group involved.* Users of copper, for example, took less aggregate action in 1984 than users of steel, but their effort was much larger in relation to their overall resources. This was a factor in President Ronald Reagan's decision to reject import relief for copper that year, in the same month that he approved new protection for steel.

Given the US government's standing concern with alliance solidarity and genuine beliefs in the national benefits of trade, visible political opposition encourages those politicians and officials to resist protection proposals. Exceptions are sometimes made for products for which a President had previously made a campaign promise, but proposals that clearly contravene US international obligations have less chance of acceptance, regardless of domestic political opposition. Still other factors probably shape trade decisions in general, macroeconomic conditions in particular. But they do not do much to explain the outcomes of the 14 episodes we have studied.

The level of future anti-protection activity will be determined by such factors as *trade dependence,* economy-wide and sector-specific, *threats to trade* in the form of new protection proposals, and a range of secondary influences such as those summarized above. It will also depend, however, on how effectively public and private actors respond to and mobilize the anti-protection interests, currently and potentially active. So we move now to draw broader recommendations from this study for the conduct of trade politics—within the United States and other trading nations.

Recommendations

If the analysis in this book is correct, what future strategies or tactics does it suggest? On the one hand, those who seek more complete and reliable import protection can find some useful information here. But our purpose is not to clear paths in that direction. Rather, we seek to draw implications from our study to stimulate the thinking of those US government officials, legislators, journalists, other citizens, and citizens of other countries who are disturbed by the recent trend toward greater protection and erosion of the General Agreement on Tariffs and Trade (GATT) system, and those who seek negotiations to reduce existing trade restrictions.

For such an audience, this study contains much *good news*—there are many special trade-dependent groups in the American economy that act against protection. There are still others who have an interest in doing so. Cumulatively, they would form an impressive force in support of more open trade.

But with this good news comes *bad news*—it is hard to pull this "force" together. Since these are "special interests," they lack a central political organization to speak for them. For the same reason, their interest is not in "free trade" as economic doctrine or ideological principle, but in the specific product flows to which they are party. They can settle for special arrangements: steel users protecting *their* sources of supply through allotments within the 1984 "voluntary" export restraints. And when attention turns away from targeted, protection-seeking campaigns to broad, trade-expanding enterprises, there is the ever-present free-rider problem: interests can profit from the results without mobilizing politically, and the payoff may be insufficiently direct or predictable to justify heavy investments of time and organization.

Expanding on the good news, the standing capacity for political action in the United States is now much larger than in the past. An enlarged body of interest group representatives is available to bring pressure to bear on *both* sides of trade issues, of course, but it does mean that those who seek to build political coalitions opposing protection have more to work with than in the past. A smaller, but growing core of "political entrepreneurs" have experience in leading such coalitions, and each campaign gives a few more their baptism of fire. Some of the Washington offices and their colleagues across the country now have more experience in anti-protection politics than they had in the past, and they regard some of that effort as having been successful. To this extent they may be more likely to participate in future efforts than in the past.

The downside is that organizing efforts may nevertheless face substantial obstacles, in addition to expense:

● A particular shipper, retailer, import user, or exporter may not depend sufficiently on the goods or foreign country to be restricted to induce it to act, or it may lack sufficient information about its trade stakes.

● Even though one division of a given bank, company, or union would lose from protection, another division might gain from the same measure, tending to immobilize the actor politically.

● Import users may face a low price elasticity of demand for their own products, encouraging them to pass the cost of protection on to their own customers rather than going into politics.

● A particular interest group's preferences may place another political issue (including protection for itself) higher in priority, and it may see a conflict between the issues.

● Pro-protection forces may establish an image in the United States that foreign producers are unfair, or that anti-protection forces are greedy and unpatriotic, tending to suppress public opposition. This image problem may not, however, suppress financial and other private contributions.

● If a campaign for protection succeeds, it may reduce subsequent dependence on the foreign product and reduce foreign spending on US exports. If protection reduces the trade dependence of potential US anti-protection forces, it may not affect their behavior if they regard the reduction as temporary. But if they see it as permanent, they may lose their interest in opposing protection.

● The President may not provide political "cover" for anti-protection forces; that is, he may fail to help legitimize their activity, or to offer alternative measures for politicians to support in place of protection. In that circumstance, potential private and congressional actors may not venture into the fray.

Perhaps the biggest gap on the anti-protection side in recent years has been in dealing with generic trade policy, proposals that are not specific to given goods but which in practice will either increase or diminish imports. Advocates of restrictions have turned increasingly to framing their proposals in generic form, out of frustration from their inability to win approval for more direct measures. For example, the steel industry worked hard to modify the antidumping law's provisions that govern whether an industry qualifies for relief. Here the problems of information and "free-riding" are at their most acute for the opponents of restrictions. Such legislation is typically highly technical; its effects will surely reach sectors beyond those intended by the proponents; and yet no one can know with certainty whose interests will be affected and to what extent. And by definition, because the proposal is generic, most of those who would benefit from defeating the idea would reap most of that benefit whether they joined the fight or not.

What sorts of action could counter these obstacles while exploiting the new political potential of anti-protection interests? The concluding pages of this book suggest some answers to this broad question.

PUBLICIZING THE SPECIFIC COSTS OF PROTECTION

First of all, there is a need to educate particular interests to their stakes in international trade. Analyses of the *general* costs of trade restrictions to American consumers, or to the economy as a whole, have become standard (and useful) fare in trade debates. But *specific* costs should be highlighted as well. The next campaign for import protection, whatever the product involved, will threaten the interests of other US economic sectors, directly or indirectly. But many of these people will not be aware of their own interests in a particular bill in Congress or complaint before the US International Trade Commission (USITC), especially not the groups less directly affected. Up to the present, a major constraint on political participation on the anti-protection side, in product-specific episodes, has been that many companies, unions, cities, and others who have a special interest in that particular trade decision have not been fully informed of their own interests in time to make a difference.

This study suggests simple techniques—examining export data, input-output tables, and the like—for identifying who, besides the obvious household consumer, has interests at stake in a given episode, as well as identifying who among them has the greatest political potential. Organizations disturbed by protection could monitor specific proposals and use techniques like these to identify potential opposition coalitions tailored to these proposals. Some could write privately and directly to the interested groups, reporting their findings—simply the "hard, cold fact" that "you could be hurt if this measure is adopted." A few activists have used these steps in scattered past episodes as shown above. More could do it more often.

Experience suggests that some recipients who would not act otherwise, will act politically on this sort of information. And when this results, say, in stimulating genuine constituent appeals to Congress, members notice. Some of the interests more directly affected, who may be aware of the issue, may be preoccupied with other issues, or feel pulled in more than one direction, or may even be organized by pro-protection forces—as was the Consumer Federation of America on the domestic content bill. But appeals from the "anti" side may encourage these organizations to remain silent or to oppose the campaigns. We have reported examples of such effects—both companies working within their industry associations to dilute or defeat restrictive proposals before they emerge publicly, and others working more directly with government.

Given that the general public, and not only special interests, pays a price for protection, politicians and officials could consider whether the national government might play a greater role in improving the public information on which an effective democratic political process depends. At present, the detailed information the government collects and publishes in product cases typically ignores the interests that would be hurt by protection, and therefore is biased against them. In addition to quite properly analyzing the injury that trade causes to certain US interests, *the USITC, for example, should also calculate and include in its "injury" analyses a look at the sectors likely to be most hurt by the protection the "injured" industry seeks*. It should be required to do so in any case in which the Commission finds injury from imports.[1]

Similarly, congressional committees considering protective legislation should adopt a policy of asking the Congressional Budget Office to make similar calculations, and these estimates should be published in any committee report recommending legislation that could have a protective effect. These estimates should name specific industries, not only broad categories of the economy, that would likely suffer costs from the import restriction contemplated.

---

1. Alternatively, as one of us suggested elsewhere, a Trade Barrier Assessment Agency could be established to analyze protection's costs. I. M. Destler, *American Trade Politics: System Under Stress* (Washington and New York, NY: Institute for International Economics and Twentieth Century Fund, 1986), p. 220.

At the very least, our leaders should avoid taking any new steps that would move farther in the opposite direction. Unfortunately, the legislative trend over the past decade has been to narrow officials' discretion to take into account interests other than those of import-competing producers. Legislative proposals currently moving forward on Capitol Hill would bar even the *President*, not just the USITC, from considering all US interests in a balanced fashion as the basis for deciding for or against trade protection. Not only would such a prohibition produce poor trade policy directly, it risks, by narrowing the public definition of what is at stake in such cases, seriously retarding the spread of understanding about trade dependence in the United States, and hence political activity on behalf of more open trade policy.

The need to publicize costs of protection is certainly not peculiar to the United States. Indeed, in many other countries policymaking is much less transparent, and the costs of protection are thus much harder to calculate, let alone publicize, in a timely fashion. Steps of the sort recommended here, therefore, are all the more urgent.

ANNOUNCING RETALIATION TARGETS IN ADVANCE

As a useful part of such an information effort to improve public decisions, *governments could make known, in advance, which products of other countries would be chosen for retaliation in the event that the government decided that trade retaliation was necessary.* Such retaliation does occur sometimes, and it seems difficult to justify keeping the affected interests in ignorance until too late for them to speak out on their own behalf. And this study suggests that when other countries' retaliatory threats or actions are specific by product, rather than vague statements, targeted groups are more likely to oppose their own government's protective policy than otherwise. In the United States, wheat growers and soybean producers each pressed Washington vigorously to avoid measures that would produce or prolong disputes with China and the European Community (EC).

The obvious risk of using coercive threats against the United States is that they might inflame American resentment even more, and provoke a trade conflict that in the end harmed the exporting country more than the United States. This risk is most obvious to smaller countries highly dependent on the United States for military support or markets. There is no assurance that damage, if it occurred, could be contained within the realm of commerce.

So such an approach might be most effective if undertaken by nations that are themselves important economic powers.

But the purpose of a retaliatory threat is to achieve results without having to implement the threat. And if threats, by the US government as well as by others, routinely specified in advance the people that would feel the pain, it is conceivable that governments would need to carry them out less often than otherwise. Such an advance announcement might energize anti-protection political activity in the target country, putting pressure on its government to make the compromises necessary for settlement of the specific trade dispute. And over time, routine advance notice by both sides might eventually change domestic politics in both countries in the direction of greater balance.

More concretely, all governments that were willing could—either by agreement or in parallel—publish annually a list of likely retaliation targets for each of their major trading partners. In a given dispute, a revised list might be necessary as well. In the United States, such a requirement for advance notification could be made statutory under section 301 of the Trade Act of 1974, or another law.

The case of US retaliation against Japan over semiconductors in the spring of 1987 illustrates that affected interests do react to specific threats. In this case, notice was not given until the decision to employ trade sanctions had essentially been made. Thus the decision itself was not really subject to influence. Nonetheless, when the list of candidate products was released, no fewer than 74 US producers streamed to the Department of Commerce hearings, to object to targeting specific goods that they needed to import. General Electric, for example, testified that certain refrigerator parts were "of a kind obtainable only from Japan."[2]

FORMING TRANSNATIONAL ALLIANCES FOR MARKET OPENING

None of these anti-protection devices need be limited to the American market. Other countries have different political institutions, but certainly import protection imposed by West Germany, Brazil, or Japan imposes costs on special interests there. The US government and US firms should continue to encourage overseas users and importers of American products to press for market opening within their political systems, on the model of the foreign

---

2. *Journal of Commerce*, 13 June 1987.

role in Washington anti-protection coalitions. Moreover, foreign governments interested in open and reciprocal trade ought to encourage such coalitions as a counterweight to entrenched protectionist forces. In Japan, for example, the Prime Minister has sought market opening but faced strong, special-interest resistance; he would benefit from stronger political pressure from the anti-protection side.

Some critics complain about foreign participation in our domestic trade policy process—prestigious law firms serving Japanese clients, the EC, or Korean firms, or the Canadian Ambassador working Capitol Hill. Our judgment is to the contrary—we believe such transnational political influence is a natural, even desirable, consequence of economic interdependence. In the United States, it can help alert Americans to their own dependence on specific trade flows. *But anti-protection politics, like trade liberalization, works best when it is reciprocal.* Americans should be equally involved in the struggle for open markets abroad.

KEEPING UNFAIR TRADE PRACTICES IN PERSPECTIVE

The United States—and other countries too—should recognize the important political dilemma raised by the issue of unfair trade. On the one hand, international rules and national laws assure victims of such practices of their right to compensation. Appeals for antidumping duties, countervailing duties on subsidized imports, and other measures are clearly legitimate when applied according to agreed rules. Genuinely unfair practices are not likely to disappear overnight, nor will the need for remedies.

On the other hand, the growing tendency of US petitioners and politicians to seek import relief by alleging unfair foreign practices clearly suppresses anti-protection political activity, whether the claim is legitimate in a given case or not, by spreading the view that foreigners are "cheating" or that importing is in some sense unpatriotic. The exercise of the legal process has the political effect of unbalancing the political debate that leaders hear. The appeal of these allegations to deeply held American concerns about "fairness" is one of the reasons they invite disproportionate use.

Perhaps the best approach for leaders in the United States and other countries is to continue to emphasize that unfair foreign practices account, at most, for only a small share of their industries' problems in foreign and home markets. The most effective remedies for trade imbalances and lack of competitiveness are proper macroeconomic policies at the national level and improving productivity at the firm level. We should continue to attack unfair practices openly, but by serious enforcement of agreed international norms. We should avoid unilateral actions to create controversial new norms. For Americans, this risks mirror image legislation abroad that would imperil our own exports, at a time when we are beginning to right our trade balance; it would, in the words of one critic, "lock the barn door when the horse is trying to get back in." And at home, steps that encourage disproportionate use of "unfair trade" remedies risk driving supporters of trade expansion out of the political arena.

CREATING MORE TRADE-SPECIFIC GROUPS

One limitation of anti-protection activity comes when the consciousness or the priorities of affected interests are elsewhere: consumers on product safety, farmers on domestic legislation, businesses on regulation or taxation. A useful means of countering this tendency has been to create trade-specific lobbying groups. Among trade-specific organizations established during the period covered by our study are the Retail Industry Trade Action Coalition (RITAC) and Consumers for World Trade (CWT).

Such organizations cannot, of course, ensure priority to trade among their constituencies—CWT has never represented the mainline consumer groups, and RITAC is constrained by the local orientation of department store managements. Nonetheless, organizations with a specific trade mission and a permanent, expert staff can clearly be sources of energy and leadership in Washington trade battles.

Other anti-protection interests might consider creating similar trade-specific organizations. The greatest present gap is that of *import users,* who are intermittently engaged on specific products but lack a central focus for political activity. Whether one could be organized on an economy-wide basis is unclear, but groups might well be organized for broad product areas—basic materials (steel, copper), electronic inputs, etc. Another possibility would be greater cooperative activity by name-brand importers such as The Gap, Inc.; Nike; and Esprit.

STRENGTHENING THE ALTERNATIVES TO PROTECTION

In the battle against trade barriers, it remains hard to beat something with nothing. Those who oppose import restrictions need alternatives to offer those suffering the costs of open trade. The President and his chief advisers need other things to give legislators and private groups, in order to help win them to the anti-protection side, or at least convince them to stay on the sidelines.

Many presidents have negotiated trade barrier reductions abroad, in order to reward exporters for their domestic support for US trade liberalization, and also as a rationale to resist demands for new protection at home. But other forms of assistance to industries suffering from import competition will help reduce the pressures that make anti-protection campaigns necessary, and help members of Congress act so as to harvest net gains from trade. To this end, a revived program of trade adjustment assistance is essential.[3]

Such a program must be thought of as part of a more comprehensive set of adjustment policies, aiming to help workers (and other resources) within the domestic economy move into internationally competitive enterprises. One reason why organized labor, for example, has been increasingly pro-protection is that many of its workers are in industries that see only pain, and not gain, from trade. But exporting and import-using firms like Caterpillar, Inc., employ unionized workers also. The more that labor moves into enterprises with growing national and global sales prospects, the less will its interests be served by trade protection. Certain workers will inevitably suffer when the structure of economic activity changes, as it must if firms (and nations) are to keep their competitive positions. But it would be neither fair policy nor good trade politics to make labor bear this burden alone.

INVITING PARTICIPATION BY AFFECTED INDUSTRIES

The President's trade policy managers could make more frequent use of grass-roots tactics illustrated occasionally in this study, such as those of former trade representatives Robert S. Strauss and William E. Brock. The USTR is in a unique position to act as the builder of political coalitions in support of a basically open trade posture, if the President backs him or her when necessary. The USTR negotiates with foreign counterparts to get benefits for his constituents, and meanwhile he must also bargain with American groups to get their support for international agreements, and their

---

3. Gary Clyde Hufbauer and Howard F. Rosen, *Trade Policy for Troubled Industries*, POLICY ANALYSES IN INTERNATIONAL ECONOMICS 15 (Washington: Institute for International Economics, March 1986); Robert Z. Lawrence and Robert E. Litan, *Saving Free Trade: A Pragmatic Approach* (Washington: Brookings Institution, 1986).

opposition to restrictive measures that can torpedo his overseas deals. Yet mechanisms like the USTR's private-sector advisory groups were not, for the most part, employed effectively in product episodes.

US Trade Representatives can use their sectoral advisory committees to inform and stimulate potential supporters. By including representatives of potential anti-protection interests on these committees, they can ensure that the advice they receive is balanced. In return, industry representatives get a special, inside view of what Washington is thinking and doing. And when a domestic political battle must be fought, these representatives are then relatively well informed about the broader national and international implications, as well as their narrower company or union concerns.

Officials can informally encourage affected interests to express their concerns openly or confidentially to members of Congress and colleagues in the private sector. A request from the White House is not likely to cause a company or union to do something it views as contrary to its interests, but such a high-level appeal can indeed cause a sympathetic group to shift its priorities to international trade matters for a time, when it otherwise would have worked on another issue.

Private firms and associations should consider making more use of their grass-roots networks on behalf of their interests in international trade. The trend in US politics is toward greater mobilization of individual constituents to write letters, make telephone calls, or even personal visits to their representatives on policy issues. Large firms are increasingly developing computerized mailing lists of their stockholders, employees, and retirees, for political purposes. And despite the well-known free-rider problem and the expense of electronic and direct-mail technologies, this study documents instances in which such techniques have been used in opposition to import protection, and in which political representatives have reported being favorably impressed. These include struggles over textiles in 1983 and 1985, and over shoes in 1984 and 1985, for example. When delegations of car or shoe dealers meet with their senator, they typically have a much greater effect than a visit by a Washington lobbyist. Those who seek protection will certainly continue to use these techniques.

PLANNING FOR RATIFICATION OF THE URUGUAY ROUND AGREEMENTS

Finally, all those interested in the possibilities of international negotiations to liberalize world trade, including the Uruguay multilateral round begun in

December 1986, need to be interested in political forces like those studied here. In order to receive concessions abroad, it is normally necessary to make concessions in return, such as reductions in one's own restrictive practices, of which the United States now has an ample supply. But such concessions, however necessary at the international table, will meet political opposition at home, from the groups benefiting from the measures. Such opposition could doom proposed future agreements, even if they would bring gains to the United States economy taken as a whole.

So planning for trade negotiations requires planning for the ratification phase. At that stage, the negotiator will need domestic allies, groups ready to speak out on behalf of the package, and to oppose crippling amendments, giving members of Congress the confidence to vote to ratify in the face of opposition.

Studies of international trade negotiations generally stress the key role played by export interests, with their potential gains providing some political offset to the costs paid by import-competing groups. In this sense, the declining trade dependence of US exporters in 1980–85, and the apparent relative fall-off in their political activity, is a poor harbinger for the new round. This is one more reason why it is important, mainly through nontrade measures, to achieve a marked improvement in the US trade balance. As this emerges, we can expect export interests to become resurgent political forces as well.

But one should not forget the interests on the import side. Users and retailers gain from trade liberalization as well, and while they may never mobilize as fully as the industries suffering from imports, they may actually represent more workers—substantially more in some cases. Their activity can provide at least a partial offset, increasing the political leeway of negotiators seeking further market opening at home and overseas.

The Anti-Protection Research Agenda

We close with some thoughts for other scholars. Like any effort to open up a new subject, this study has reached for more than it can grasp. Its method has proved sufficient to highlight a range of apparent causes of anti-protection activity, and to establish a link between political action and policy decision. But much more could usefully be done:

- Studies ought ideally to *survey pro-protection as well as anti-protection activity*, comparing their magnitudes, sources, and impacts in particular product battles and more generally.

• Future research should *reach deeper into anti-protection activity on generic trade issues.* We have probed enough here to suggest strikingly different patterns of interest group involvement, changes over time, etc., but a comprehensive treatment of such issues could further test our tentative conclusions here, and suggest new ones.

• Parallel studies ought to be taken of *anti-protection politics in other major trading nations.* Analogous techniques of analysis could be employed to identify potential anti-protection groups, and assess their political activity and impact in Bonn, Brasilia, Paris, or Tokyo.

• Studies could usefully include more policy episodes, perhaps dating back as far as the 1960s, in order to provide a fuller test of persuasive theses not substantiated by the data gathered here: for example, those relating policy outcomes to unemployment, the exchange rate, or the trade balance.

In these and other ways, scholarship could usefully expand on the research and conclusions presented here. Anti-protection activity is an *important, understudied* phenomenon in trade politics. With this book and others, however, that second adjective need no longer apply.

Appendices

Appendix A   Group Political Activity in Product-Specific Episodes

This appendix reports evidence on which groups acted and to what extent in each episode, and on the techniques by which the evidence was collected and classified. This information is the basis for constructing aggregate activity scores used in chapters 3 and 5 and for the quantitative tests discussed in chapter 4 and appendix C.

This appendix is provided also as a means of simplifying the citation of sources in the text of the study. Here, each organization found to be active or inactive is named. These results are based on systematic searches of five types of source, and the merging and crosschecking of thousands of pieces of evidence:

● published reports of the US International Trade Commission (USITC), showing who testified in opposition to petitions for import relief

● published hearings of the US Congress showing who testified or sent letters in opposition to protection

● periodical indexes and key newspapers and magazines, specifically, *New York Times, Washington Post, Wall Street Journal, Journal of Commerce, Congressional Quarterly Weekly Report, National Journal, Public Affairs Information Service,* and *F&S International*

● 51 personal interviews with participants in the political coalitions and policy decisions discussed, including current and former executive branch officials, members of Congress and staff, Washington group representatives, and company executives

● in a few cases, documents released by anti-protection groups in support of their positions; for example a joint letter to the President showing the names of the signatories.

Ideally, every fact should be linked to a specific set of references, but such a presentation in this study would be extremely cumbersome. Many of these facts can be verified from public sources. Personal interviews are essential both for amplifying on the membership of coalitions and degrees of their activity, especially lobbying, and interpreting the meaning of the other facts. These interviews were conducted with a promise of confidentiality so that those sources unfortunately cannot be identified precisely.

Although we are confident that we did not overlook any substantial activity reported in the public sources we checked, we are not equally sanguine regarding evidence on behind-the-scenes activity. Individuals involved in various episodes may well have knowledge of activity or inactivity different from what we present here. Undoubtedly, there will be differences of opinion over the way in which we have assigned the activity rankings. Nevertheless, we applied a consistent methodology in each case—albeit one inherently limited by our primary reliance on public sources—and we believe it has provided us with a data base sufficient to draw some reasonable conclusions regarding anti-protection activity.

The appendix is divided into tables, one for each of the 14 episodes described in chapter 2. The groups found to be active in each case are then classified by type of group—exporter, retailer, foreign private or government group, consumer, importer, or general organization—and level of activity—heavy, moderate, light, or none.

The tables also include the activity rating given each group. The default ratings are as follows: 0 for no activity, 1 for light activity, 5 for moderate activity, and 25 for heavy activity. Generally, greater activity means committing more resources and taking more risks of creating enemies. Light activity is defined as some combination of the following: the actor signs a joint letter along with other organizations (1 point); it writes on its own (including letters published with congressional hearings) (2 points); a press release is issued, individual constituents may send scattered communications to officials. Any activity greater than signing a joint letter was generally rated as a 2 or 3.

Moderate activity is defined as some combination of the following: the group testifies before a congressional committee or the USITC (one appearance = 4 points; two or three appearances, or one appearance plus two to three written submissions = 5 points; four or more appearances = 6 points); hires a law firm or public relations firm to represent it; lobbies officials selectively; makes limited efforts to stimulate constituent contacts with Washington; provides limited technical assistance to its official friends in preparing policy proposals or compiling supporting evidence; finances a study to show the effects of the proposed protection (7 or more points for limited lobbying or other activity in addition to testimony).

Heavy activity is defined as many of the steps mentioned above plus some combination of the following: the group lobbies many members of Congress and executive officials; organizes thousands of letters and personal visits by constituents; spends hundreds of thousands of dollars; works frequently and closely with official friends in developing strategies and proposals, providing detailed supporting evidence of potential job losses; plays a lead role in coalition meetings, which are held every week or two during the most intense phases. A foreign government may threaten retaliation. Foreign companies may substitute financing for visible activity. Foreign actors may lobby potential allies in American society rather than US officials directly.

The data base also includes groups that might be expected to be active, but for which no evidence of activity was found. In all cases (except sugar, see chapter 3), sectors whose exports to the major targeted countries were more than 3 percent of total production were included. Also included were the American Farm Bureau Federation and National Grange, and four major umbrella business groups—Emergency Committee for American Trade, National Association of Manufacturers, Business Roundtable, and Chamber of Commerce of the United States—in all cases. In addition, the activity summaries include the American Association of Exporters and Importers in all cases as the main representative of importers and the International Longshoremen's Association, the American Association of Port Authorities, and National Association of Stevedores in all cases as representatives of service industries that would be adversely affected by import restrictions. The major consumer organizations are also consistently listed: Consumers Union, Consumer Federation of America, Consumers for World Trade, and the League of Women Voters (because they were active in more than one case in conjunction with consumer groups). Finally, in cases in which we found evidence of activity by private foreign groups, but not by their governments, we included the governments under no activity (country names alone indicate government activity, private foreign groups are named specifically where possible).

In cases involving imported inputs, sectors for which the input was more than 25 percent of total costs (10 percent in the case of sugar) were included. The tables listing these groups, and the specific export sectors included in each case may be found in appendix B. In cases involving consumer goods, the summaries include applicable retailer groups; for example, the National Automobile Dealers Association in the auto cases; and the National Retail Merchants Association in the footwear and textile and apparel cases.

TABLE A.1   **Autos 1980–81**

Type of group	Actor	Rating
	HEAVY ACTIVITY	
	None	
	MODERATE ACTIVITY	
Exporters	American Soybean Assn.	5
	General farm groups	5
Retailers	American International Auto Dealers Assn.	10
Foreign private	Toyota Motor Sales USA, Inc.	5
or government	Nissan Motor Corp., USA	5
groups	Subaru of America	5
	American Honda Motor Co.	5
	Honda Motor Co., Ltd., and Honda of America	4
	Alfa Romeo	4
	BMW of North America	4
	Fiat of North America	4
	Mercedes Benz of North America	4
	Peugeot Motors of America	4
	Saab-Scania of America, Inc.	4
	Volvo of America	4
	Renault USA, Inc.	4
	Japanese Automobile Manufacturers Assn.	4
Consumers	Consumers for World Trade	5
	Center for Auto Safety	4
Importers	Automobile Importers of America	7
Umbrella or	US Council for an Open World Economy	5
general	Council for a Competitive Economy	5
organizations		

Type of group	Actor	Rating
	LIGHT ACTIVITY	
Consumers	Consumers Union	2
General	Coalition of importers, consumers, and farmers	9
	NO ACTIVITY	
Exporters	Softwood logs	0
	Coal	0
	Aircraft industry	0
Retailers	National Auto Dealers Assn.	0
Foreign private	France	0
or government	Italy	0
groups	Germany	0
	Sweden	0
	Japan	0
Consumers	Consumer Federation of America	0
	League of Women Voters	
Importers	American Assn. of Exporters and Importers	0
Umbrella or	Business Roundtable	0
general	Chamber of Commerce	0
organizations	Emergency Committee for American Trade	0
	National Association of Manufacturers	0
Service	International Longshoremen's Assn.	0
organizations	National Assn. of Stevedores	0
	American Assn. of Port Authorities	0

TABLE A.2   **Autos 1982–83**

Type of group	Actor	Rating
	HEAVY ACTIVITY	
Retailers	American International Auto Dealers Assn.	25
Foreign private	Toyota Motor Sales USA, Inc.	25
or government	American Honda Motor Co.	15
groups	Nissan Motor Corp., USA	15
Umbrella or general organizations	Chamber of Commerce	20
	MODERATE ACTIVITY	
Exporters	Caterpillar Tractor	6
	IBM	5
	National Corn Growers Assn.	6
	National Assn. of Wheat Growers	5
	American Soybean Assn.	6
	National Grange	7
Retailers	National Auto Dealers Assn.	10
Foreign private or government groups	Volkswagen of America	5
Consumers	Consumers for World Trade	6
	League of Women Voters	5
	Council for Advancement of Consumer Policy	4
Importers	Auto Importers of America	10
	American Assn. of Exporters and Importers	8
	Ford Motor Co.	3
	General Motors	5
Service organizations	American Assn. of Port Authorities	6
	Port Authority of New York and New Jersey	5
	Port of Portland, Oregon	5
	National Assn. of Stevedores	5
	International Longshoremen's Assn.	5

Type of group	Actor	Rating
	MODERATE ACTIVITY	
Umbrella or	National Foreign Trade Council	8
general	Emergency Committee for American Trade	5
organizations	National Assn. of Manufacturers	6
	Asia-Pacific Council of American Chambers	
	of Commerce	4
	Developing World Industry and Technology, Inc.	4
	LIGHT ACTIVITY	
General	Coalition of 22 associations	22
Exporters	Boeing Corp.	2
	Aerospace Industries Assn. of America	3
	National Council of Farmer Cooperatives	3
	National Farmers Union	1
	American Farm Bureau Federation	1
	National Broiler Council	3
	Semiconductor Industry Assn.	2
	Tubexpress Systems	2
	American Electronics Assn.	1
	Computer and Business Equipment Manufacturers	
	Assn.	1
	Continental Grain Co.	1
	International Hardwood Products Assn.	1
	Lockheed Corp.	1
	Millers National Federation	1
	National Grain Trade Council	1
	National Soybean Processors Assn.	1
	Poultry and Egg Institute of America	1
	Scientific Apparatus Makers Assn.	1
	Rice Millers Assn.	1
	Xerox Corp.	1
	American Paper Institute	1
	Grain Sorghum Producers Assn.	1
	National Turkey Federation	1

TABLE A.2 **Autos 1982–83**

Type of group	Actor	Rating
	LIGHT ACTIVITY (*cont.*)	
Retailers	American Retail Federation	1
	Footwear Retailers of America	1
	National Retail Merchants Assn.	1
Consumers	Consumers Union	1
	American Assn. of Retired Persons	1
	Washington Citizens for World Trade	1
Foreign private or government groups	American Izusu Motors, Inc.	2
	European Community	2
Service organizations	Jacksonville Maritime Assn.	2
	Philadelphia Port Corp.	2
	Delaware River Port Authority	1
	Massachusetts Port Authority	1
	National Customs Brokers and Freight Forwarders Assn.	1
	Port of Baltimore	1
Umbrella or general organizations	Business Roundtable	2
	US Council for an Open World Economy	2
	International Trade Council	2
	Council for a Competitive Economy	2
	US Council for International Business	1
	Pacific Rim Trade Assn.	1
Unidentified	Certainteed Corp.	1
	Colonial Sugar Co.	1
	Imperial Sugar Co.	1
	International Apple Institute	1
	International Assn. of Ice Cream Manufacturers	1
	Milk Industry Foundation	1
	US Cane Sugar Refiners Assn.	1
	Beatrice Food Co.	1
	Direct Selling Assn.	1
	FMC Corp.	1
	MFA, Inc.	1

Type of group	Actor	Rating
	NO ACTIVITY	
Exporters	Coal industry	0
	Softwood logs	0
Foreign private	Japan	0
or government	Germany	0
groups		
Consumers	Consumer Federation of America	0

TABLE A.3 **Copper 1984**

Type of group	Actor	Rating
	HEAVY ACTIVITY	
Users	National Electrical Manufacturers Assn.	25
Foreign private or government groups	Chile	25
	MODERATE ACTIVITY	
Users	CERRO Copper Products Co.	4
	Southwire Co.	4
	Copper and Brass Fabricators Council	5
Foreign private or government groups	Canada	5
	Mexico	5
	Peru	5
	Zaire	5
	Zambia	5
	Rio Tinto Zinc Corp. (British-owned)	4
	LIGHT ACTIVITY	
Exporters	National Assn. of Wheat Growers	2
	Council of Farmer Cooperatives	1
	American Farm Bureau Federation	1
	US Wheat Associates	1
	Corn growers	1
Foreign private or government groups	Philippines	2
	Organization of American States	2
	Australia	1
	NO ACTIVITY	
Exporters	Piston-type internal combustion engines	0
	Coal industry	0
	Rice growers	0
	Motor vehicle parts	0
	Motor vehicles	0
	National Grange	0
Users	Bronze and brass makers	0
Consumers	Consumer Federation of America	0

Type of group	Actor	Rating
	NO ACTIVITY	
	Consumers Union	0
	League of Women Voters	0
	Consumers for World Trade	0
Umbrella or	Business Roundtable	0
general	Chamber of Commerce	0
organizations	Emergency Committee for American Trade	0
	National Assn. of Manufacturers	0
Service	International Longshoremen's Assn.	0
organizations	National Assn. of Stevedores	0
	American Assn. of Port Authorities	0
Importers	American Assn. of Exporters and Importers	0

TABLE A.4   **Footwear 1976–77**

Type of group	Actor	Rating
	HEAVY ACTIVITY None	
	MODERATE ACTIVITY	
Retailers	Volume Footwear Retailers of America	10
	American Retail Federation	4
	National Retail Merchants Assn.	5
	National Shoe Retailers Assn.	6
	Thom McAn	4
Foreign private or government groups	Taiwan Footwear Manufacturing Assn.	5
	Spanish Footwear Industry	5
	Brazilian Producers	5
	Korean Footwear Exporters and Korean Leather and Fur Exporters Assns.	5
	Mexican Producers of Footwear	5
	European Confederation of the Footwear Industry	4
	Ireland-US Council for Commerce and Industry, Inc.	5
	Italian Footwear Manufacturers Assn.	4
	Swiss Shoe Manufacturers Assn.	4
Consumers	Consumers Union	6
Importers	Adidas Athletic Footwear	4
	Bally, Inc.	4
	Scholl, Inc.	4
	Blue Ribbon Sports	4
	Trans-World Shoe Import Co., Inc.	4
	VANCO	4
	Associated Ski Boot Importers	4
	Sidney Rich Associates	4
	Regenstein's	4
	American Importers Assn.	6
Umbrella or general organizations	US Council for an Open World Economy	4
	US-Italian Chamber of Commerce	5

Type of group	Actor	Rating
	LIGHT ACTIVITY	
Exporters	National Assn. of Wheat Growers	1
	NO ACTIVITY	
Exporters	Cotton growers	0
	Soybean growers	0
	Semiconductor manufacturers	0
	Corn growers	0
Retailers	Volume Shoe Corp.	0
	K-Mart	0
Consumers	Consumer Federation of America	0
	League of Women Voters	0
Umbrella or	Business Roundtable	0
general	Chamber of Commerce	0
organizations	Emergency Committee for American Trade	0
	National Assn. of Manufacturers	0
Service	International Longshoremen's Assn.	0
organizations	National Assn. of Stevedores	0
	American Assn. of Port Authorities	0

TABLE A.5   **Footwear 1984–85**

Type of group	Actor	Rating
	HEAVY ACTIVITY	
Retailers	Footwear Retailers of America	25
Foreign private	South Korea	25
or government	European Community	20
groups		
	MODERATE ACTIVITY	
Exporters	Agriculture in general	5
Retailers	Volume Shoe Corp.	6
	K-Mart	5
	National Retail Merchants Assn.	4
	National Shoe Retailers Assn.	5
Foreign private	Brazil	7
or government	Taiwan Footwear Manufacturers Assn.	5
groups	Mexican National Footwear Chamber of Commerce	
	(and three footwear producer assns.)	5
	Argentina	5
	Aris and Isotoner, Inc. (Philippines)	4
Importers	Nike	6
	Puma	6
	Adidas	6
	Clossco	4
	Hughesco	4
	Libco	4
	VANCO	4
	Pony Sports Leisure, Inc.	4
	American Assn. of Exporters and Importers	6
	International Footwear Assn.	4
	Fashion Footwear Assn. of New York	4

Type of group	Actor	Rating
	LIGHT ACTIVITY	
Exporters	National Assn. of Wheat Growers	2
Retailers	Retail Industry Trade Action Coalition	2
Consumers	Consumers for World Trade	1
Importers	Elan Imports	2
Umbrella or general organizations	US Council for an Open World Economy	2
	NO ACTIVITY	
Exporters	Aircraft industry	0
	Coal industry	0
	Electrical components, semiconductors	0
	Hides	0
Foreign private or government groups	Mexico	0
	Philippines	0
	Taiwan	0
Consumers	Consumer Federation of America	0
	Consumers Union	0
	League of Women Voters	0
Umbrella or general organizations	Business Roundtable	0
	Chamber of Commerce	0
	Emergency Committee for American Trade	0
	National Assn. of Manufacturers	0
Service organizations	International Longshoremen's Assn.	0
	National Assn. of Stevedores	0
	American Assn. of Port Authorities	0

T A B L E A.6   **Steel 1977–78**

Type of group	Actor	Rating
	HEAVY ACTIVITY	
	None	
	MODERATE ACTIVITY	
Users	Tempel Steel Co.	4
	Independent Wire Producers Assn.	5
Importers	American Institute for Imported Steel	6
	West Coast Metal Importers Assn.	4
Service	Assn. of Steel Distributors	5
organizations	Steel Service Center	4
	LIGHT ACTIVITY	
Users	General Electric	1
Foreign private	Japan Iron and Steel Exporters Assn.	2
or government	European Community	2
groups		
	NO ACTIVITY	
Exporters	Coal industry	0
	Soybean growers	0
	Aircraft industry	0
	Instruments to measure electricity	0
	Corn growers	0
	Wheat growers	0
	Tobacco growers	0
	Softwood logs	0
	Office machines	0
	Electric components	0
	Organic chemicals	0
	American Farm Bureau Federation	0
	National Grange	0
Users	Motor vehicles	0
	Motor vehicle parts	0
	Metal cans	0
	Barrels, drums, and pails	0
	Prefabricated metal buildings	0

Type of group	Actor	Rating
	NO ACTIVITY	
	Automotive stampings	0
	Steel springs	0
	Metal partitions	0
	Fabricated plate work	0
	Architectural metal work	0
	Railroad equipment	0
	Bearings	0
	Construction machinery and equipment	0
	Crowns and closures	0
	Transportation equipment, n.e.c.	0
	Turbines	0
	Metal stampings, n.e.c.	0
	Screw machine products	0
	Fabricated structural steel	0
	Valve Manufacturing Assn.	0
Foreign private or government groups	Japan	0
Consumers	Consumer Federation of America	0
	Consumers Union	0
	League of Women Voters	0
Umbrella or general organizations	Business Roundtable	0
	Chamber of Commerce	0
	Emergency Committee for American Trade	0
	National Assn. of Manufacturers	0
Service organizations	International Longshoremen's Assn.	0
	National Assn. of Stevedores	0
	American Assn. of Port Authorities	0
	Crispin (trader)	0
Importers	American Assn. of Importers	0

n.e.c.   not elsewhere classified.

TABLE A.7   **Steel 1982**

Type of group	Actor	Rating
	HEAVY ACTIVITY	
Foreign private or government groups	European Community	25
	MODERATE ACTIVITY	
Users	Combustion Engineering, Inc.	4
	Foster Wheeler Corp.	4
Foreign private or government groups	Brazilian steel companies	5
	Romanian steel company	4
	Japanese steel company	4
	Spanish Steel Producers Assn.	4
	Korean Iron and Steel Institute	5
	LIGHT ACTIVITY	
Users	West coast fabricators	1
Foreign private or government groups	Korea Economic Institute	1
	Japan Steel Information Center	1
Consumers	Consumers for World Trade	1
Importers	American Institute for Imported Steel	1
	Minimills	1
	NO ACTIVITY	
Exporters	Animal feed	0
	Soybeans growers	0
	Aircraft industry	0
	Coal industry	0
	Scientific instruments	0
	Corn growers	0
	National Grange	0
	American Farm Bureau Federation	0
Users	Prefabricated metal buildings	0
	Metal cans	0
	Barrels, drums, and pails	0
	Automotive stampings	0

Type of group	Actor	Rating
	NO ACTIVITY	
	Steel springs	0
	Fabricated wire products	0
	Metal partitions	0
	Fabricated plate work	0
	Architectural metal work	0
	Fabricated structural steel	0
	Sheet metal work	0
	Motor vehicles	0
	Motor vehicle parts	0
	Railroad equipment	0
	Bearings	0
	Construction machinery and equipment	0
	Crowns and closures	0
	Transportation equipment, n.e.c	0
	Turbines	0
	Metal stampings, n.e.c	0
	Industrial fasteners	0
Foreign private or government groups	Brazil	0
	Romania	0
	South Korea	0
	Japan	0
Consumers	Consumer Federation of America	0
	Consumers Union	0
	League of Women Voters	0
Umbrella or general organizations	Business Roundtable	0
	Chamber of Commerce	0
	Emergency Committee for American Trade	0
	National Assn. of Manufacturers	0
Service organizations	International Longshoremen's Assn.	0
	National Assn. of Stevedores	0
	American Assn. of Port Authorities	0

n.e.c.   not elsewhere classified.

T A B L E A.8   **Steel 1984**

Type of group	Actor	Rating
	HEAVY ACTIVITY	
User/exporter	Caterpillar Tractor	25
Foreign private	European Community	25
or government	Canada	25
groups	South Korea	25
	MODERATE ACTIVITY	
Exporters	American Soybean Assn.	7
	Land of Lincoln Soybean Assn.	4
	Sporting Goods Manufacturers Assn.	4
Users	Alliance Wall Corp.	4
	American Wire Producers Assn.	5
	Hack and Band Saw Manufacturing Assn.	4
	Davis Lynch, Inc.	4
	INA Bearing Co.	4
	The Torrington Co.	4
	Tubular Corp. of America	5
	Pinole Point Steel Co.	5
	California Steel Co.	4
	Kaiser Steel Co.	4
	West Coast Ad Hoc Steel Wire Producers Committee	5
	Pacific Steel	5
	Berg Steel Pipe Co.	5
	General Electric Co.	4
	R. Hoe and Co.	4
	Steel Products Manufacturing Committee	4
	Jackson Forge Corp.	4
	J.B. and S. Lees, Ltd.	4
	Simonds Cutting Tools	4
Foreign private	Brazil	6
or government	Mexican steel producers	5
groups	Swedish Iron Masters Assn.	5
	Venezuela	5
	Argentina	5
	Spanish Steel Producers Assn.	4

Type of group	Actor	Rating
	MODERATE ACTIVITY	
	Japan Iron and Steel Exporters Assn.	5
	John Lysaght, Ltd. (Australia)	5
	Taiwan Iron and Steel Industry Assn.	5
	South African steel producer	4
Consumers	Consumers for World Trade	6
Importers	American Institute for Imported Steel	7
	West Coast Metal Importers Assn.	5
	Ohio River Steel Corp.	5
	Nucor Co.	4
Service Groups	Assn. of Steel Distributors	4
	Steel Service Center Institute	4
	LIGHT ACTIVITY	
Exporters	National Grange	2
	National Assn. of Wheat Growers	2
	National Corn Growers Assn.	1
	American Farm Bureau Federation	1
	Millers National Federation	1
	National Grain Trade Council	1
	North American Export Grain Assn.	1
	Cargill	1
	Rice Millers Assn.	1
	Island Creek Coal Co.	2
	Aerospace Industries Assn. of America	1
Users	Anti-Friction Bearing Manufacturers Assn.	2
	Construction Industry Manufacturing Assn.	2
	3M Corp.	1
	Hardware Manufacturers Assn.	2
	Superior Metal Products	2
	Steel Shipping Container Institute	2
	Trailer Hitch Manufacturing Assn.	1
	American Metal Stamping Assn.	2
	Steel USA	1
	American Hoist and Derrick Co.	1

TABLE A.8 **Steel 1984**

Type of group	Actor	Rating
	LIGHT ACTIVITY	
	Barber-Greene Co.	1
	Draw-Tite, Inc.	1
	Durable, Inc.	1
	Eaz-Lift Spring Co.	1
	Evans Cooperage Co.	1
	Federal Pipe and Supply Co.	1
	Fleetwood Enterprises	1
	Genesee Fence and Supply Co.	1
	Gilmore Steel Corp.	1
	Gomaco Co.	1
	Great Lake Fence Co.	1
	UNIT Crane and Shovel Co.	1
	Security Fence and Supply	1
	TRW	1
	General Motors	2
Retailers	Retail Industry Trade Action Coalition	1
Importers	American Assn. of Exporters and Importers	1
Service organizations	American Assn. of Port Authorities	1
	National Assn. of Stevedores	2
Umbrella or general organizations	US Council for an Open World Economy	2
	Business Roundtable	1
	NO ACTIVITY	
Exporters	Nonpiston-type internal combustion engines	0
	Specified acyclic organic chemicals	0
	Instruments to measure electricity	0
Users	Metal cans	0
	Prefabricated metal buildings	0
	Fabricated structural steel	0
	Goodyear	0
	Railroad equipment	0
	Crown and closures	0

Type of group	Actor	Rating
	NO ACTIVITY	
	Architectural metal work	0
	Transportation equipment	0
	Turbines	0
	Industrial fasteners	0
Foreign private	Mexico	0
or government	Sweden	0
groups	Spain	0
	Japan	0
	Australia	0
	Taiwan	0
	South Africa	0
Consumers	Consumer Federation of America	0
	Consumers Union	0
	League of Women Voters	0
Umbrella or	Chamber of Commerce	0
general	Emergency Committee for American Trade	0
organizations	National Assn. of Manufacturers	0
Service	International Longshoremen's Assn.	0
organizations		

TABLE A.9 **Sugar 1974**

Type of group	Actor	Rating
	HEAVY ACTIVITY	
	None	
	MODERATE ACTIVITY	
Users	Coca-Cola	5
	Sugar Users Group	5
Consumers	National Consumer Congress	6
	LIGHT ACTIVITY	
Consumers	League of Women Voters	1
Umbrella or general organizations	Committee for a National Trade Policy	2
	NO ACTIVITY	
Users	US Cane Refiners Assn.	0
	National Confectioners Assn.	0
Consumers	Consumer Federation of America	0
	Consumers Union	0
Umbrella or general organizations	Business Roundtable	0
	Chamber of Commerce	0
	Emergency Committee for American Trade	0
	National Assn. of Manufacturers	0
Service organizations	International Longshoremen's Assn.	0
	National Assn. of Stevedores	0
	American Assn. of Port Authorities	0

TABLE A.10 **Sugar 1978–79**

Type of group	Actor	Rating
	HEAVY ACTIVITY	
Users	US Cane Refiners	15
Consumers	Consumers Against Sugar Hikes	15
	MODERATE ACTIVITY	
Users	Sugar Users Group	10
	Milk Industry Foundation and International Assn. of Ice Cream Makers	6
Foreign private or government groups	Central American Council	6
	LIGHT ACTIVITY	
Users	Independent Bakers Assn.	1
	Refined Syrups and Sugars, Inc.	1
Consumers	Consumers for World Trade	2
Service organizations	Sugar Workers Council of America	1
	International Longshoremen's Assn.	1
Foreign private or government groups	Mauritius Sugar Syndicate	2
	Organization of American States	2
	Sugar Assn. of Caribbean	2
	Redpath Sugars of Canada	2
Importers	New York Sugar and Coffee Exchange	2
Umbrella or general organizations	US Council for an Open World Economy	4
	NO ACTIVITY	
Users	National Confectioners Assn.	0
Foreign private or government groups	Swaziland	0
	Mauritius	0
	Canada	0
Consumers	Consumers Union	0
Umbrella or general organizations	Business Roundtable	0
	Chamber of Commerce	0
	Emergency Committee for American Trade	0
	National Assn. of Manufacturers	0
Importers	American Assn. of Exporters and Importers	0
Service organizations	National Assn. of Stevedores	0
	American Assn. of Port Authorities	0

T A B L E A.11   **Sugar 1981–82**

Type of group	Actor	Rating
	HEAVY ACTIVITY	
Users	US Cane Sugar Refiners Assn.	20
	MODERATE ACTIVITY	
Users	Sugar Users Group	10
Foreign private or government groups	Dominican Republic	6
Consumers	Consumers Federation of America	5
Umbrella or general organizations	US Council for an Open World Economy	4
	LIGHT ACTIVITY	
Foreign private or government groups	Producing member countries of the International Sugar Arrangement	1
	Australia	1
	Organization of American States	1
	NO ACTIVITY	
Users	National Confectioners Assn.	0
Consumers	Consumers Union	0
	League of Women Voters	0
	Consumers for World Trade	0
Umbrella or general organizations	Business Roundtable	0
	Chamber of Commerce	0
	Emergency Committee for American Trade	0
	National Assn. of Manufacturers	0
Importers	American Assn. of Exporters and Importers	0
Service organizations	International Longshoremen's Assn.	0
	National Assn. of Stevedores	0
	American Assn. of Port Authorities	0

TABLE A.12   **Textiles 1983**

Type of group	Actor	Rating
	HEAVY ACTIVITY	
Exporters	Wheat growers	20
Foreign private or government groups	China	25
	MODERATE ACTIVITY	
Retailers	Retailers in general	5
	LIGHT ACTIVITY	
Exporters	American Soybean Assn.	1
Consumers	Consumers in general	1
	NO ACTIVITY	
Exporters	Leather	0
	Softwood logs	0
	Cotton	0
	American Farm Bureau Federation	0
	National Grange	0
Retailers	National Retail Merchants Assn.	0
	American Retail Federation	0
	K-Mart	0
	Dayton-Hudson	0
	May Department Stores	0
Consumers	Consumer Federation of America	0
	Consumers Union	0
	League of Women Voters	0
	Consumers for World Trade	0
Umbrella or general organizations	Business Roundtable	0
	Chamber of Commerce	0
	Emergency Committee for American Trade	0
	National Assn. of Manufacturers	0
Importers	American Assn. of Exporters and Importers	0
Service organizations	International Longshoremen's Assn.	0
	National Assn. of Stevedores	0
	American Assn. of Port Authorities	0

TABLE A.13   **Textiles 1984**

Type of group	Actor	Rating
	HEAVY ACTIVITY	
Retailers	Retail Industry Trade Action Coalition	20
Foreign private or government groups	China	20
	Hong Kong	25
	MODERATE ACTIVITY	
Exporters	Wheat growers	6
Retailers	National Retail Merchants Assn.	6
Consumers	Consumers for World Trade	4
	Citizens for a Sound Economy	4
Importers	American Assn. of Exporters and Importers	10
	Marisa Christina, Inc.	4
	LIGHT ACTIVITY	
Exporters	National Grange and seven other farm groups	8
Retailers	American Retail Federation	1
	K-Mart	1
Foreign private or government groups	Group of 23	3
	Caribbean nations	1
	European Community	1
Service organizations	National Customs Brokers and Freight Forwarders Assn.	2
Importers	Mast Industries and Country Miss	1
	House of Lloyd, Inc.	2
	S. Shamash and Sons, Inc.	2
Umbrella or general organizations	Asia-Pacific Council of American Chambers of Commerce	3
	US Council for an Open World Economy	2

Type of group	Actor	Rating
	NO ACTIVITY	
Exporters	Softwood logs	0
	Fertilizers	0
	American Farm Bureau Federation	0
Consumers	Consumer Federation of America	0
	Consumers Union	0
	League of Women Voters	0
Umbrella or general organizations	Business Roundtable	0
	Chamber of Commerce	0
	Emergency Committee for American Trade	0
	National Assn. of Manufacturers	0
Service organizations	International Longshoremen's Assn.	0
	National Assn. of Stevedores	0
	American Assn. of Port Authorities	0

TABLE A.14   **Textiles 1985–86**

Type of group	Actor	Rating
	HEAVY ACTIVITY	
Retailers	Retail Industry Trade Action Coalition	25
	American Free Trade Council	25
Foreign private or government groups	Hong Kong	15
	China	25
Importers	American Assn. of Exporters and Importers	25
	MODERATE ACTIVITY	
Exporters	National Assn. of Wheat Growers	5
Retailers	J.C. Penney	5
	K-Mart	5
	The Limited, Inc.	5
Foreign private or government groups	Taiwan Textile Federation	5
	Thailand	5
Umbrella or general organizations	Northwest Apparel and Textile Assn. and Northwest Fair Trade Alliance	5
	American-Israel Chamber of Commerce and Industry	4
	American-Indonesian Chamber of Commerce	5
	Italy-American Chamber of Commerce	4
	International Trade Council	4
	Emergency Committee for American Trade	4
Consumers	Citizens for a Sound Economy	5
	Consumers for World Trade	5
Importers	Levi Strauss	5
	Liz Claiborne	4
	Paul Reed, Inc.	4
	Martin Tandler	4
	Marisa Christina, Inc., et al.	8
	Toy Manufacturers of America	4
	Nike Inc.	4
	Assn. for Contract Textiles	4
	International Silk Assn. of the United States	4

Type of group	Actor	Rating
	MODERATE ACTIVITY	
	Royal Silk, Ltd.	5
	Samsonite	4
	Farah Mfg. Co.	4
	American-Caribbean Trade Assn.	5
	LIGHT ACTIVITY	
Exporters	National Corn Growers Assn.	1
	Soybean growers	1
Retailers	Associated Merchandising Corp.	1
	National Retail Merchants Assn.	2
	Dayton-Hudson	1
	May Dept. Stores	1
	Federated Dept. Stores	1
	Zayre's	1
Foreign private	Caribbean island nations	2
or government	Korean Traders Assn.	3
groups	Invicta Group Industries, Ltd. (Australia)	2
	Bangladesh	2
	Pacific Basin countries	2
	European Community	1
Umbrella or	American Chamber of Commerce of Thailand	2
general	Bread for the World	2
organizations	California Council for International Trade	2
	Coalition to Preserve International Trade	2
Importers	Ad hoc Textile and Trade Legislation Committee	2
	Import Committee of the National Handbag Assn.	2
Service	Port Authority of New York and New Jersey	1
organizations	American President Lines	1
	Lykes Brothers	1
	Steamship Co.	1
	Sea-Land Services, Inc.	1
	United States Lines, Inc.	1
	National Customs Brokers and Freight Forwarders Assn.	1

TABLE A.14   **Textiles 1985–86**

Type of group	Actor	Rating
	NO ACTIVITY	
Exporters	Hides	0
	Cotton	0
	Fertilizers	0
	Computers	0
	Electronic components	0
	American Farm Bureau Federation	0
	National Grange	0
Consumers	Consumer Federation of America	0
	Consumers Union	0
	League of Women Voters	0
Umbrella or general organizations	Business Roundtable	0
	Chamber of Commerce	0
	National Assn. of Manufacturers	0
Service organizations	International Longshoremen's Assn.	0
	National Assn. of Stevedores	0
Foreign private or government groups	Australia	0
	South Korea	0
	Taiwan	0

Appendix B   *Identifying Anti-Protection Interests and Estimating Political Potential*

This appendix presents both the raw data used to identify sectors that might be expected to oppose proposals for protection, and the calculations performed in estimating the political potential—the resources available for mobilization—of those groups. The most directly affected sectors were the focus in each case: industrial users of imported inputs in cases involving intermediate goods; retailers in cases involving consumer goods; and exporters in all but the sugar cases (for reasons explained in chapter 3). As noted in chapter 3, only those exporters for whom sales to the targeted foreign countries were more than 3 percent of total foreign and domestic shipments, and industrial users for whom the targeted input was more than 25 percent of final costs (10 percent in the case of sugar), were included in the data base of expected anti-protection interests.

The export sectors in the first 10 tables are ranked in descending order according to the share of exports to the target countries in total product shipments[1]. The sources for these tables are: US Department of Commerce, *US Exports,* FT 455, *U.S. Industrial Outlook,* and *Statistical Abstract of the United States,* for various years; and US Department of Agriculture, *Agricultural Statistics,* various years. The abbreviations SITC and SIC in each table stand for Standard International Trade Classification and Standard Industrial Classification, respectively. Because the product categories are determined by different groups for different purposes, the trade and production figures are not always exactly comparable. Significant differences in product coverage have been noted in individual tables, as necessary.

Tables B.11 to B.13 show the user sectors most dependent on copper, steel, and sugar, respectively. The sources for these tables are: US Department of Commerce, *The Detailed Input-Output Structure of the U.S. Economy,*

---

1. There are 10 rather than 11 exporter tables here since the table covering the 1983 textile episode B appears in chap. 3.

1977, U.S. Industrial Outlook, and *Trade and Employment,* 1984; and Data Resources, Inc., US Central Data Base.

In addition to showing the input-output coefficients for users in the steel, sugar, and copper episodes, the tables also include employment figures for those sectors, and the adjusted employment figures that are used in estimating each group's political potential in chapter 5. Very simply, for each sector above the threshold, the user coefficient was multiplied by employment in the year before the decision was made. The sum of the adjusted employment figures measures the coalition's estimated anti-protection potential. This total is then used as the denominator in the ratio of aggregate activity to potential.

T A B L E B.1   **Key US export sectors in 1980–81 autos case: major 1980 exports to Japan**

SITC	SIC	Commodity
2471	2411	Softwood logs[a]
2631	0131	Cotton
0410	0111	Wheat and wheat flour
2222	0116	Soybeans
0440	0115	Corn
3222	12	Coal
7925, 7929	3721, 3728	Aircraft and parts
6841	[b]	Unwrought aluminum and ingots
8752	[c]	Measuring and controlling instruments

a. Total exports and shipments include hardwood logs, which have averaged less than 10 percent of exports and less than 20 percent of shipments in recent years.
b. Total exports and shipments include primary aluminum and semifinished products.
c. Shipments include products in SIC categories 3811, 3822–25, 3829, 3832.

It is also arrayed against pro-protection potential in order to estimate the relative weight of the pro- and anti-protection forces in cases involving intermediate goods.[2]

Similar calculations were performed to estimate the political potential of retail interests, the most directly affected group when imports of consumer goods are threatened with restrictions. In episodes involving automobiles, footwear, and textiles and apparel, total retail employment was adjusted downward, using imports as a share of consumption as a proxy for trade dependence. The results of these calculations are presented in table B.14.

---

2. As a further refinement, similar estimates of exporters' political potential were added to the coalition totals. As noted in ch. 5, however, adding export potential did not alter the findings.

Target's share of shipments	Ratio of exports to shipments	Target's share of exports	Exports to target	Total exports	Total shipments
(percentage)			(million dollars)		
0.194	0.235	0.828	1,291	1,560	6,648
0.132	0.718	0.183	525	2,864	3,987
0.118	0.708	0.167	1,098	6,586	9,303
0.081	0.433	0.188	1,106	5,883	13,601
0.079	0.417	0.191	1,633	8,570	20,554
0.065	0.229	0.284	1,311	4,621	20,196
0.032	0.385	0.084	1,081	12,816	33,312
0.025	0.102	0.248	503	2,026	19,880
0.025	0.281	0.089	414	4,677	16,616

TABLE B.2 **Key US export sectors in 1982–83 autos case: major 1982 exports to Japan**

SITC	SIC	Commodity
0310	0190	Fish, fresh or frozen[a]
2631	0131	Cotton
2471	2411	Softwood and veneer logs[b]
2222	0116	Soybeans
3222	12	Coal
0440	0115	Corn
0410	0111	Wheat
7925, 7929	3721, 3728	Aircraft and parts
8752	c	Measuring and controlling instruments
7599		Automated data processing machine parts

n.a.   not available.
a. Shipment value is based on the ex vessel value of the domestic catch.
b. Total exports and shipments include hardwood logs, which have averaged less than 10 percent of exports and less than 20 percent of shipments in recent years.
c. Shipments include products in SIC categories 3811, 3822–25, 3829, 3832.

TABLE B.3 **Key US export sectors in 1984 copper case: major 1983 exports to Chile, Canada, Peru, Zambia, Zaire**

SITC	SIC	Commodity
7843	3714	Motor vehicle parts
4220		Rice
7810	3711	Motor vehicles
3222	12	Coal
0410	0111	Wheat
7925	3721	Airplanes
7239	3531, 3532	Construction and mining machinery parts[a]
0440	0115	Corn
7135		Piston-type internal combustion engines
7599		Automated data processing machinery parts

n.a.   not available.
Note: Because exports to Canada swamp those to the other target countries, a slightly different methodology has been used in this case. The top five exports to Canada and the top five to the other countries combined are the export sectors included here.
a. Shipments include final assembled products as well as parts.

178

Target's share of shipments	Ratio of exports to shipments	Target's share of exports	Exports to target	Total exports	Total shipments
	(percentage)			(million dollars)	
0.163	0.237	0.689	390	566	2,390
0.147	0.573	0.256	501	1,955	3,410
0.124	0.176	0.706	829	1,174	6,668
0.078	0.501	0.156	971	6,240	12,463
0.067	0.260	0.257	1,525	5,934	22,850
0.059	0.258	0.227	1,290	5,683	22,039
0.057	0.680	0.084	564	6,676	9,813
0.024	0.329	0.074	848	11,522	35,024
0.022	0.241	0.093	460	4,955	20,539
n.a.	n.a.	0.100	396	3,964	n.a.

Targets' share of shipments	Ratio of exports to shipments	Targets' share of exports	Exports to targets	Total exports	Total shipments
	(percentage)			(million dollars)	
0.111	0.169	0.654	5,175	7,916	46,776
0.048	0.849	0.057	43	754	888
0.042	0.047	0.907	3,864	4,258	90,935
0.040	0.182	0.221	886	4,008	22,070
0.036	0.717	0.050	306	6,121	8,533
0.016	0.211	0.073	409	5,570	26,377
0.014	0.301	0.048	156	3,281	10,911
0.006	0.479	0.012	75	6,480	13,537
n.a.	n.a.	0.733	1,092	1,490	n.a.
n.a.	n.a.	0.137	683	5,000	n.a.

TABLE B.4 **Key US export sectors in 1976–77 footwear case: major 1976 exports to Spain, Brazil, Taiwan, Korea**

Schedule B	SIC	Commodity
2631	0131	Cotton
0410	0111	Wheat
2214	0116	Soybeans
7293	3674	Electronic tubes and semiconductors[a]
0440	0115	Corn
7341, 7349	3721, 3728	Aircraft and parts
3214	12	Coal
5120	2865, 2869	Organic chemicals
7221	b	Electric power machinery
724	3661–62, 3651	Telecommunication apparatus
2820	5093	Iron and steel scrap

n.a. not available.
a. Shipments of semiconductors only.
b. Shipments include products in SIC categories 34433, 34436, 3511, 3612, 3621.

TABLE B.5 **Key US export sectors in 1984–85 footwear case: major 1984 exports to Korea, Taiwan, Brazil, Spain, Italy**

SITC	SIC	Commodity
2111	3111	Hides[a]
2631	0131	Cotton
2222	0116	Soybeans
0410	0111	Wheat
0440	0115	Corn
3222	12	Coal
7925, 7929	3721, 3728	Aircraft and parts
7768	3671, 3674	Electronic tubes and semiconductors
8752	b	Measuring and controlling instruments
7599		Automated data processing machinery parts

n.a. not available.
a. Based on Department of Commerce estimate that exports of hides accounted for 69 percent of those available from that year's slaughter.
b. Shipments include products in SIC categories 3811, 3822–25, 3829, 3832.

180

Targets' share of shipments	Ratio of exports to shipments	Targets' share of exports	Exports to targets	Total exports	Total shipments
(percentage)			(million dollars)		
0.108	0.322	0.330	350	1,049	3,255
0.096	0.660	0.146	565	3,880	5,868
0.050	0.378	0.130	435	3,315	8,776
0.047	0.291	0.160	270	1,671	4,292
0.030	0.387	0.130	407	5,223	13,524
0.022	0.364	0.061	374	6,116	16,825
0.020	0.217	0.090	274	2,910	13,399
0.017	0.133	0.130	381	2,928	22,026
0.016	0.133	0.120	158	1,343	10,126
0.011	0.094	0.114	228	1,997	21,232
n.a.	n.a.	0.374	237	634	n.a.

Targets' share of shipments	Ratio of exports to shipments	Targets' share of exports	Exports to targets	Total exports	Total shipments
(percentage)			(million dollars)		
0.251	0.690	0.364	426	1,171	1,697
0.208	0.667	0.312	761	2,441	3,658
0.103	0.477	0.216	1,175	5,438	11,402
0.101	0.741	0.136	880	6,477	8,735
0.051	0.345	0.148	1,048	7,081	20,544
0.039	0.170	0.227	927	4,090	24,000
0.033	0.266	0.124	1,312	10,612	39,929
0.032	0.187	0.169	635	3,762	20,133
0.021	0.059	0.357	545	1,526	25,955
n.a.	n.a.	0.092	596	6,446	n.a.

TABLE B.6   Key US export sectors in 1977–78 steel case: major 1976 exports
to the EC and Japan

Schedule B	SIC	Commodity
2214	0116	Soybeans
1210		Tobacco, unmanufactured
0440	0115	Corn
2422	2411	Softwood logs
0410	0111	Wheat
3214	12	Coal
0813	a	Oilseed cake and meal
7149	357	Office machinery, n.e.c.[b]
7295	3822–25, 3829	Instruments to measure electricity[c]
7341, 7349	3721, 3728	Aircraft and parts
7293	3671	Electronic tubes, n.e.c.[d]
5120	2865, 2869	Organic chemicals
7184	3531, 3532	Construction and mining machinery parts[e]
7328	3714	Motor vehicle parts

n.e.c.   not elsewhere classified.
a. Shipments based on 1976 export unit value of $197 per ton for soybean meal and cake, 95 percent of total shipments.
b. Shipments include all office machines and parts.
c. Shipments include nonelectric instruments.
d. Shipments include all electronic components other than semiconductors.
e. Shipments include machinery, as well as parts.

Targets' share of shipments	Ratio of exports to shipments	Targets' share of exports	Exports to targets	Total exports	Total shipments
	(percentage)			(million dollars)	
0.253	0.378	0.671	2,223	3,315	8,776
0.237	0.383	0.618	569	921	2,404
0.192	0.386	0.496	2,591	5,223	13,524
0.155	0.170	0.911	776	852	5,000
0.140	0.661	0.211	820	3,880	5,868
0.129	0.217	0.595	1,731	2,910	13,399
0.103	0.171	0.602	541	899	5,265
0.090	0.158	0.568	1,123	1,978	12,487
0.078	0.171	0.456	483	1,060	6,181
0.077	0.364	0.212	1,295	6,116	16,825
0.062	0.210	0.295	493	1,671	7,959
0.059	0.133	0.443	1,297	2,928	22,026
0.045	0.243	0.183	515	2,815	11,562
0.016	0.175	0.093	474	5,079	29,024

TABLE B.7   **Key US export sectors in 1982 steel case: major 1981 exports to EC**

SITC	SIC	Commodity
0810		Animal feed
2222	0116	Soybeans
7925, 7929	3721, 3728	Aircraft and parts
3222	12	Coal
8752	a	Measuring and controlling instruments
0440	0115	Corn
7239	3531–2	Construction and mining machinery parts
7843	3714	Motor vehicle parts
5173	2865, 2869	Specified acyclic organic chemicals[b]
7526		Input-output storage machines
7599		Automatic data processing machine parts
7149		Nonpiston engine parts

n.a.   not available.
a. Shipments include products in SIC categories 3811, 3822–25, 3829, 3832
b. Shipments include all industrial organic chemicals.

Target's share of shipments	Ratio of exports to shipments	Target's share of exports	Exports to target	Total exports	Total shipments
(percentage)			*(million dollars)*		
0.367	0.629	0.583	1,598	2,739	4,354
0.231	0.516	0.446	2,768	6,200	12,005
0.101	0.407	0.247	3,588	14,499	35,618
0.100	0.270	0.372	2,162	5,805	21,514
0.086	0.271	0.317	1,577	4,968	18,348
0.056	0.397	0.142	1,135	8,014	20,200
0.038	0.250	0.150	673	4,485	17,923
0.021	0.217	0.099	859	8,717	40,215
0.014	0.056	0.257	576	2,245	40,060
n.a.	n.a.	0.503	1,490	2,964	n.a.
n.a.	n.a.	0.477	1,800	3,774	n.a.
n.a.	n.a.	0.524	943	1,798	n.a.

TABLE B.8   Key US export sectors in 1984 steel case: major 1983 exports to
EC, Japan, Korea, Canada

SITC	SIC	Commodity
2631	0131	Cotton
0810	a	Animal feed stuff
2222	0116	Soybeans
0440	0115	Corn
7149	3159 [b]	Nonpiston-type internal combustion engine pts.
3222	12	Coal
8752	c	Measuring and controlling instruments
7843	3714	Motor vehicle parts
7925, 7929	3721, 3728	Airplanes and parts
7810	3711	Motor vehicles
5173	2865, 2869	Specified acyclic organic chemicals[d]
7526		Input-output storage machines
7135, 7139		Piston-type internal combustion engs. and pts.
7599		Automated data processing machines and parts

n.a.   not available.
a. Shipments are of feed crops less corn.
b. Shipments are of internal combustion engines, not elsewhere classified.
c. Shipments include products in SIC categories 3811, 3822–25, 3829, and 3832.
d. Shipments include all industrial organic chemicals.

Targets' share of shipments	Ratio of exports to shipments	Targets' share of exports	Exports to targets	Total exports	Total shipments
(percentage)			(million dollars)		
0.477	0.731	0.653	1,186	1,817	2,486
0.473	0.607	0.779	2,183	2,802	4,615
0.287	0.464	0.619	3,667	5,925	12,775
0.218	0.479	0.455	2,947	6,480	13,537
0.152	0.217	0.702	1,343	1,913	8,813
0.145	0.182	0.796	3,190	4,008	22,070
0.131	0.227	0.576	2,758	4,785	21,107
0.129	0.169	0.761	6,023	7,916	46,776
0.119	0.301	0.396	4,724	11,917	39,548
0.043	0.047	0.929	3,955	4,258	90,935
0.030	0.056	0.540	1,134	2,101	37,284
n.a.	n.a.	0.708	2,338	3,300	n.a.
n.a.	n.a.	0.691	2,190	3,171	n.a.
n.a.	n.a.	0.682	3,412	5,000	n.a.

TABLE B.9   **Key US export sectors in 1984 textile case: major 1983 exports to Hong Kong and China**

SITC	SIC	Commodity
0410	0111	Wheat
2471	2411	Softwood logs[a]
5629	2873	Fertilizers, n.s.p.f.[b]
0440	0115	Corn
1222	2111	Cigarettes
8752	[c]	Measuring and controlling instruments
7925, 7929	3721, 3728	Aircraft and parts
5881	2821	Synthetic resins
7764	3674	Integrated circuits[d]
7599		Automated data processing machine parts

n.a.   not available; n.s.p.f.   not specifically provided for.

a. Includes hardwood logs, which have averaged less than 10 percent of exports and less than 20 percent of shipments in recent years.

b. Imports of fertilizers under SITC 5629 are other than phosphatic; shipments under SIC 2873 are of nitrogenous fertilizers.

c. Includes shipments under SIC categories 3811, 3822–25, 3829, 3832.

d. Shipments are of semiconductors and related devices.

Targets' share of shipments	Ratio of exports to shipments	Targets' share of exports	Exports to targets	Total exports	Total shipments
	(percentage)			(million dollars)	
0.047	0.763	0.061	397	6,509	8,533
0.032	0.166	0.195	229	1,175	7,074
0.031	0.113	0.273	100	366	3,236
0.012	0.479	0.024	158	6,480	13,537
0.011	0.094	0.120	135	1,126	11,941
0.009	0.227	0.038	183	4,785	21,107
0.008	0.301	0.028	332	11,917	39,548
0.008	0.119	0.069	174	2,510	21,053
0.008	0.340	0.023	102	4,352	12,801
n.a.	n.a.	0.051	255	5,000	n.a.

TABLE B.10 **Key US export sectors in 1985 textile case: major 1984 exports to Hong Kong, Korea, Taiwan, China**

SITC	SIC	Commodity
2111	3111	Hides[a]
2631	0131	Cotton
0410	0111	Wheat
5629	2873	Fertilizers, n.s.p.f.[b]
2222	0116	Soybeans
0440	0115	Corn
7768	3671, 3674	Electronic tubes and semiconductors
7925, 7929	3721, 3728	Aircraft and parts
8752	c	Measuring and controlling instruments
7599		Automated data processing machinery parts

n.a. not available; n.s.p.f. not specifically provided for.
a. Estimate based on Department of Commerce data showing that exports accounted for 69 percent of hides available from that year's slaughter.
b. Imports are of fertilizers other than phosphatic; shipments are for nitrogenous fertilizers.
c. Includes shipments under SIC categories 3811, 3822–25, 3829, 3832.

TABLE B.11 **Users of copper: dependence, employment, and political potential** (thousand employees)

I-O	SIC	Copper user	Copper coefficient	1983 employment	Adjusted employment
38.0700	3351	Rolling and drawing	0.542	25.5	13.8
38.1000	3357	Nonferrous wire drawing and insulating	0.257	78.9	20.3
38.1200	3339	Brass, bronze, and copper castings	0.255	14.1	3.6
38.0500	3399	Primary nonferrous metals, n.e.c.	0.249	9.0	2.2
38.0900	3356	Nonferrous rolling and drawing, n.e.c.	0.139	19.9	—
37.0402	3399	Primary metal products, n.e.c.	0.132	10.7	—
40.0200	3432	Plumbing fixture fittings and trim	0.113	24.4	—

— not applicable; n.e.c. not elsewhere classified.

Targets' share of shipments	Ratio of exports to shipments	Targets' share of exports	Exports to targets	Total exports	Total shipments
(percentage)			(million dollars)		
0.229	0.690	0.331	388	1,171	1,697
0.191	0.667	0.287	700	2,441	3,658
0.114	0.741	0.154	997	6,477	8,735
0.094	0.348	0.271	360	1,330	3,826
0.051	0.477	0.106	579	5,438	11,402
0.037	0.345	0.107	755	7,081	20,544
0.034	0.187	0.179	675	3,762	20,133
0.020	0.266	0.075	792	10,612	39,929
0.019	0.059	0.328	500	1,526	25,955
n.a.	n.a.	0.078	500	6,446	n.a.

TABLE B.12   **Users of steel: dependence, employment, and political potential**
(thousand employees)

I-O	SIC	Commodity	Steel coefficient
40.0902	3449	Miscellaneous metal work	0.526
40.0901	3448	Prefabricated metal buildings	0.497
39.0200	3412	Metal barrels, drums, and pails	0.490
41.0201	3465	Automotive stampings	0.466
42.0700	3493	Steel springs, except wire	0.432
39.0100	3411	Metal cans	0.394
40.0500	3441	Fabricated structural steel	0.393
41.0100	345	Screw machine products (including nuts and bolts)	0.372
42.0500	3495–6	Miscellaneous fabricated wire products	0.345
61.0300	3743	Railroad equipment	0.339
23.0500	2542	Metal partitions and fixtures	0.317
59.0302	3714	Motor vehicle parts and accessories	0.300
49.0200	3562	Ball and roller bearings	0.298
40.0600	3443	Fabricated plate work	0.291
40.0700	3444	Sheet metal work	0.290
45.0100	3531	Construction machinery and equipment	0.283
41.0202	3466	Crowns and closures (bottle caps)	0.271
40.0800	3446	Architectural metal work	0.270
61.0700	3799	Transportation equipment, n.e.c.	0.255
43.0100	3511	Turbines and turbine generators	0.253
41.0203	3469	Metal stampings, n.e.c.	0.251

n.e.c.   not elsewhere classified.
a. Denotes 1982 employment.

	Employment			Adjusted employment	
1977	1981	1983	1977	1981	1983
16.3	17.9	21.4[a]	8.6	9.4	11.2
22.7	24.4	23.5[a]	11.3	12.1	11.7
12.4	12.0	12.1	6.0	5.9	5.9
132.4	95.1	86.9	61.7	44.3	40.5
8.2	5.2	5.0	3.5	2.3	2.2
59.8	50.3	49.5	23.6	19.8	19.5
99.3	115.6	76.8	39.0	45.4	30.2
104.7	110.9	85.5	39.0	41.2	31.8
54.1	43.7	64.2	18.7	15.0	22.2
56.2	48.6	34.5	19.1	16.5	11.7
28.0	26.6	27.9	8.9	8.4	8.8
450.7	359.4	339.1	135.2	107.8	101.7
50.6	53.3	43.4	15.1	15.9	12.9
123.5	115.8	105.3	35.9	33.7	30.6
77.4	81.4	81.6	22.5	23.6	23.7
155.3	145.9	82.5	44.0	41.3	23.4
7.9	7.1	6.7	2.1	1.9	1.8
20.8	24.4	27.0	5.6	6.6	7.3
10.3	8.6	8.6	2.6	2.2	2.2
40.9	36.5	36.3	10.3	9.2	9.2
103.2	112.8	99.8	25.9	28.3	25.0

194 ANTI-PROTECTION

TABLE B.13 Users of sugar: dependence, employment, and political
potential (thousand employees)

I-O	SIC	Commodity	Sugar coefficient
14.1900	2062	Refiners	0.383
14.2800	2087	Flavoring extracts and syrups, n.e.c.	0.202
14.2200	2086	Bottled and canned soft drinks	0.106
14.2002	2066	Chocolate and cocoa products	0.088
14.2001	2065	Confectionary products	0.084
14.1403	2045	Blended and prepared flour	0.083
14.1402	2043	Cereal breakfast foods	0.062
14.2003	2067	Chewing gum	0.059
14.1802	2052	Cookies and crackers	0.054

— not applicable; n.e.c. not elsewhere classified.
a. Since data on employment in refineries cannot be broken down between those refining imported and those refining domestic cane sugar, we excluded refiner employment from our calculations of political potential (on either the pro- or anti-protection side, see chapter 5).

TABLE B.14 Retail interests: dependence, employment, and political
potential (thousand employees)

Case	Import market share	Employment	Adjusted employment
Autos 1980–81	0.35	759.3	265.7
Autos 1982–83	0.36	695.7	250.5
Footwear 1976–77	0.29	281.2	82.7
Footwear 1984–85	0.54	307.4	166.1
Textiles 1983	0.12	1,992.0	243.0
Textiles 1984	0.14	2,002.0	272.0
Textiles 1985–86	0.17	2,100.0	365.4

Employment			Adjusted employment		
1973	1978	1981	1973	1978	1981
10.6	10.3	9.4	a	a	a
10.2	11.6	10.9	2.1	2.3	2.2
117.0	115.1	117.3	12.4	12.2	12.4
10.6	10.0	19.5	—	—	—
60.7	56.3	55.1	—	—	—
8.1	9.0	7.6	—	—	—
13.1	16.6	15.6	—	—	—
7.0	6.6	5.8	—	—	—
41.9	47.3	46.5	—	—	—

Appendix C   Determinants of Anti-Protection Activity: Logit Estimates

An exploratory effort to test a few of the hypotheses presented in chapter 4 indicates that several are promising for identifying conditions favorable and unfavorable for anti-protection activity. The results of this first look are presented as a supplement to other kinds of evidence, and as an impetus toward further research. They do not, at this stage, offer a basis for firm conclusions.

The primary unit of observation is a particular interest group's degree of activity or inactivity in one of the 14 episodes. Each group found to have acted in any episode is added to a pool of observations. Also added are groups expected to be active in a given episode but actually inactive, as far as our evidence indicates. All US export sectors highly dependent on the trade at issue—those that shipped 3 percent or more of their total output to the particular countries whose own products would be restricted in a given episode—are listed for that episode, either as active or inactive. All import-using sectors for which the imported input equals or exceeds 25 percent of output value (10 percent in the case of sugar) are listed as either active or inactive in episodes involving intermediate goods. Appropriate retailer groups are included as either active or inactive in cases involving consumer goods. Certain groups with more general commercial or policy interests in trade also consistently appear in each episode. An importer, port community, general commercial organization (for example, the Chamber of Commerce) or nonprofit interest group that acts against protection in one episode is listed as either active or inactive in all other episodes. The complete list of groups in this pool is presented in appendix A.

An ordinal dependent variable was constructed to represent degrees of political activity. A rating scheme was used to assign to each group a score increasing from 0 in proportion to the degree of the group's activity, as defined in chapter 3 and explained in appendix A. Initially, scores of 1, 5, and 25 are assigned for light, moderate, and heavy activity respectively, and

modifications are made to reflect further variations. For the present exercise, the activity scores are reduced to nine possible values.
A total of six independent variables appear in the models to follow.

• *Trade dependence:* for exporters, the proportion of total product shipments exported to target countries, and for import users, the share of steel, copper, or sugar in the total cost of their final product (as shown in the tables in appendix B); for consumers and retailers, the ratio of imports to US consumption of autos, footwear, and textiles and apparel, as appropriate; Data are not included for multisectoral commercial associations, nonprofit organizations, port authorities, and other political participants; thus, this indicator applies to only about half of the full sample of observations that have values on all other variables.

• *Inflation:* measured as the annual rate in the year prior to the political decision, based on the producer price index for exporters, retailers, and general groups, the consumer price index for consumers, and the wholesale price of the input in question for user groups.

• *Dollar exchange rate:* measured as the average real effective exchange rate[1] for eight quarters prior to the year in which the decision was made. This indicator reflects the differential between inflation rates in the United States and the rest of world, as well as nominal exchange rates, and rises when the dollar gains in value vis-à-vis other currencies.

• *Import penetration (defined for import users only):* the ratio of imports to production of the industry's final output in the year prior to the decision.

• *Unfair trade charges:* a dummy variable set equal to 1 for all groups in an episode in which protection was sought under an unfair trade statute or involved other administrative action against alleged unfair trade (as with the rules changes in the 1984 textile case), and 0 otherwise.

• *Foreign retaliation (defined for exporters only):* a dummy variable set equal to 1 for all export groups in an episode in which there was a direct, explicit act or threat of retaliation by the government of a country threatened by US import restrictions, and 0 otherwise.

---

1. Real effective exchange rates are taken from John Williamson, *The Exchange Rate System,* 2nd ed. rev., POLICY ANALYSES IN INTERNATIONAL ECONOMICS 5 (Washington: Institute for International Economics, June 1985), table A.1.

Models for political activity are then estimated using this polychotomous dependent variable and the multinomial logit technique. This technique is more appropriate here than ordinary least squares regression analysis because logit does not require an assumption that the dependent variable is continuous, or that differences between its values represent an interval scale.

The tables below report *chi*-square statistics and *p* values for each of the parameter estimates. The *chi*-square values are analogous to *t* values for parameter significance for least-squares regression. The associated *p* values give the probability that the parameter is not significantly different from 0. Also provided are the model *chi*-square and its associated *p* value, which indicates the probability that all the regressor parameters are jointly insignificant. The model *R* is a measure of goodness of fit of the model. Its square is analogous to the *R*-bar squared statistic of least-squares regression. *R*-squared can vary between 0 and 1 with larger values indicating a better fit.

Tentative results suggest some strongly significant effects and some insignificant ones. But several important qualifications apply to any conclusions drawn from these estimates. This effort to use statistical techniques is a primitive one. No data were previously available on this type of political behavior and thus they had to be generated. Measurements have been refined through several iterations, but they could be refined further. Received theory on these phenomena is quite weak, and previous research is disparate in method and contradictory in results. These tests select only a few of the possible influences for investigation. The omission of important variables is obvious from the poor fit in all these tests; in none is it close to adequate for actual predictions. The text discusses what some of those omitted variables might be. Inclusion of omitted variables might change apparent results, as always, and so further research would be necessary before these could be accepted with confidence. Because no other means of establishing generalizations will be perfect either, however, it seems best to employ a mixture of methods, including some such as these.

In general, it seems preferable to base conclusions on the fullest sample available, and use models that include as many relevant controlling variables as possible. Table C.1 begins with the largest possible sample and all variables that can be applied to it. This sample excludes foreign actors and all other observations lacking data on a variable other than trade dependence, and includes all other actors appearing in any episode. The tentative findings show strongly significant effects for all three variables, with greater political opposition associated with slower inflation and a higher dollar. (As explained

TABLE C.1   **Full sample**
Model *chi*-square = 28.41 with 3 d.f. (− 2 log l.r.)   *P* = 0.00
    n = 583   *R* = 0.11

Variable	Beta	Standard error	Chi-square	P
Inflation	− 0.018	0.010	3.47	0.06
Dollar	0.014	0.008	3.18	0.07
Unfair	− 0.724	0.172	17.81	0.00

in chapter 4, however, these variables may be reflecting changes in political conditions that broadly paralleled the macroeconomic trends.) When imports are charged with unfair practices, anti-protection activity seems to be depressed.

Data are available on trade dependence for only about half of this full sample. Table C.2 reduces the sample to these 292 observations and presents all variables that apply here. All actors are either consumer organizations, exporters, import users, or retailers. With a model including trade dependence and the three former variables, this smaller sample indicates the same results as above for the dollar and the unfairness charge. The coefficient for inflation becomes insignificant in this model and subsample. And the coefficient for trade dependence is positive but also insignificant.

The exchange rate and inflation variables are correlated with each other in this data set, and thus models using only one of the two at a time are also estimated. With a model including dependence, the unfairness condition, and

TABLE C.2   **Full trade-dependent sub-sample, four variables**
Model *chi*-square = 19.71 with 4 d.f. (− 2 log l.r.)   *P* = 0.00
    n = 292   *R* = 0.12

Variable	Beta	Standard error	Chi-square	P
Trade dependence	0.747	0.647	1.33	0.25
Inflation	− 0.008	0.010	0.66	0.41
Dollar	0.021	0.012	3.27	0.07
Unfair	− 0.812	0.246	10.94	0.00

TABLE C.3   **Full trade-dependent sub-sample, three variables**
Model chi-square = 16.43 with 3 d.f. (−2 log l.r.)   P = 0.00

n = 292   R = 0.11

Variable	Beta	Standard error	Chi-square	P
Unfair	−0.902	0.240	14.08	0.00
Inflation	−0.018	0.009	3.64	0.06
Trade dependence	0.856	0.633	1.83	0.18

the dollar, the findings for those variables are basically the same as in table C.2. Table C.3, however, shows that inflation appears significant, as in the full sample, when the dollar variable is excluded, but becomes insignificant when the dollar is added.

Thus, as noted above, this preliminary analysis leaves some ambiguities that could be resolved only with further research. For instance, it is difficult to say whether the difference in inflation results between the first two tables is due to loss of half the full sample or some other reason. And of course, whether effects would remain the same after controlling also for omitted variables is also speculative.

The remaining tables pertain to still more restricted samples, in order to explore relationships among particular types of anti-protection actors. The next reflects only import users, primarily to investigate whether greater penetration by imports in competition with their outputs changes their opposition to protection against their imported inputs. Controlling for four other variables, as in table C.4, greater import competition seems to lead, on balance, to significantly greater political opposition. This result holds up under various combinations of control variables.

Finally, it seems interesting to know whether foreign threats to retaliate against the United States impel US exporters to campaign more vigorously against the proposed US import barrier. Such threats were made in six recent episodes, but many have not identified specifically which US industries would suffer the effects of the sanctions. Table C.5 indicates that the presence of this type of threat has no effect discernible from the political behavior of all exporters in the episode.

The most important next step in the refinement of this type of evidence would be to add a comparable measure of political pressure in favor of increased protection in each episode. Eventually, even a set of simultaneous

TABLE C.4   **Import users only**
Model *chi*-square = 57.44 with 5 d.f. (− 2 log l.r.)   P = 0.00

n = 95   R = 0.41

Variable	Beta	Standard error	Chi-square	P
Trade dependence	− 0.871	2.061	0.18	0.67
Inflation	0.029	0.021	1.85	0.17
Dollar	0.188	0.043	19.52	0.00
Unfair	− 2.931	0.944	9.63	0.00
Import penetration	2.705	1.566	2.98	0.08

TABLE C.5   **Exporters only**
Model *chi*-square = 7.16 with 4 d.f. (− 2 log l.r.)   P = 0.128

n = 89   R = 0.0

Variable	Beta	Standard error	Chi-square	P
Trade dependence	4.039	2.827	2.04	0.15
Dollar	0.012	0.026	0.21	0.64
Unfair	− 1.137	0.527	4.66	0.03
Retaliation	0.038	0.626	0.00	0.95

equations representing multiple sides or parties to these interactions might be estimated. In addition, a variety of hypotheses not tested here, some of which are suggested in the text, could be developed and tested, perhaps improving on the model specifications used in this exploration.

Appendix D   Rating Policy Changes

Chapter 5 explores the effects of anti-protection activity on US trade policy. It asks, for example, whether the policy outcome tends to be correlated with the extent of such political opposition, or the occupation that dominates in that coalition. Therefore, some means of contrasting policy outcomes is needed.

Table 5.1 rates policy decisions as either reductions in protection, no change, slight increases in protection, substantial increases, or sharp increases. Distinctions among the last three categories reflect judgments about new trade-restrictive measures along two dimensions: their severity, or apparent effect on imports' share of the US market in the short run; and their rigidity, or the degree to which the form of new restrictions makes it more difficult to change them in the future, and thus contributes to their duration.

In rating the severity of a new measure, it would be desirable to compare market conditions under the new measures with market conditions that would have prevailed if restrictions had not been increased and if all other influences had had the same force. Comparing actual figures from before and after the change could be misleading, since data afterward could reflect factors other than new trade protection, such as changes in US demand, exchange rates, or supply conditions in exporting countries. An econometric trade model could help produce such a counterfactual estimate, but our resources are not sufficient to develop such a further refinement, and the result would be partly speculative even then.

Our compromise technique is to compare the actual share of US consumption supplied by imports from all sources in the year before new restraints, with their actual share during restraints. Market shares were chosen because they abstract from changes in the level of US demand. In addition, since most of the new measures applied only to certain foreign suppliers and exempted others, global imports are used in order to capture any diversion to uncovered suppliers in an assessment of relative restrictiveness from the US viewpoint.

Of the nine episodes that produced increases in protection, subsequent

202

TABLE D.1 **Judging the severity of protection**
(percentage)

Episode	Pre-restraint period	Market share of imports	Post-restraint period	Average market share of imports	Percent change in market share
Textiles 1983	1982	11.7	1983–84	14.8	+ 21
Textiles 1984	1984	17.0	1985–86	20.1	+ 18
Steel 1982	1982	21.8	1983–84	23.6	+ 8
Autos 1980–81	1980	34.7	1981–82	35.1	+ 1
Shoes 1976–77	1976	47.0	1977–78	47.1	0
Steel 1977–78	1977	17.8	1978–79	16.6	− 6
Steel 1984	1984	26.5	1985–86	24.1	− 8
Sugar 1981–82	1981	50.0	1982–83	33.7	− 33

Source: Gary Clyde Hufbauer, Diane T. Berliner, and Kimberly Ann Elliott, *Trade Protection in the United States: 31 Case Studies* (Washington: Institute for International Economics, March 1986); US Department of Commerce, *U.S. Industrial Outlook 1987,* Washington.

trade data are available for eight. Those eight outcomes tend to cluster into three groups. Imports from all sources actually enlarged their US market share in the 1983 and 1984 textiles and apparel, steel 1982, and first autos cases after the changes in trade policy. These four cases each involved restrictions on just one or two countries, however. Moreover, although changes in restrictions reduced the market share of targeted suppliers in all cases but one, sometimes severely, the leaky nature of most of the restraints permitted an increase in imports from unrestricted suppliers.

For example, the EC share of the US steel market dropped by 22 percent after restraints were imposed, even though total import market share went up by 8 percent. The textile cases showed the greatest increase in imports, even after tightening of existing restraints that are notoriously leaky, applying only to some categories from some countries. In 1983 and 1984, in fact, the increased protection was targeted at only one country (China) and two countries (Hong Kong and China), respectively. Furthermore, the real exchange rate was appreciating in much of this period and new suppliers overseas were increasing capacity in sectors like these. Thus, in those cases showing a continuing increase in imports even after new restrictions were imposed, it is likely that the increases would have been even greater had there been no new restrictions. Finally, it should be reiterated that this exercise is intended to measure relative changes in protection, not the absolute level of the final trade barriers. (A related method, focusing first on changes in only the targeted suppliers' market share, and then weighting according to the share of total imports targeted, produces the same final policy ratings.)

The final episode began in 1985 with the "Jenkins bill" designed to cut textile imports sharply. It ended in 1986 with defeat of the bill. But during the same time, President Reagan negotiated changes in US bilateral agreements with key suppliers, South Korea, Taiwan, and Hong Kong, restricting their future growth more than before, though not actually reducing imports from their levels at that time. The US administration also sought and gained changes in the international Multi-Fiber Arrangement that permit restrictions on certain additional minor fibers. We rate these negotiated changes as part of the outcome of the Jenkins bill struggle, since it seems clear that they were undertaken, at least in part, in order to persuade some members of Congress to sustain President Reagan's veto of the bill. All in all, this policy outcome is rated as most comparable to the other slight increases in protection.

These nine policy changes varied in rigidity, but the pattern does not alter a classification based only on severity. A new measure is considered least rigid if it has a statutory termination date, such as the section 201 escape clause on footwear, or is a price-based, rather than a quantitative, restriction, as under the trigger price mechanism for steel in 1977–78. At the other extreme, the 1982 sugar quotas were unilaterally imposed as a result of legislation with no set termination date. Removing them would require either an act of Congress to amend the sugar program or a willingness on the part of the administration to undertake substantial budgetary outlays to support the domestic sugar price. In between are all the other increases, which were applied by negotiation but lacked the protection of a statutory termination date. These are mostly "voluntary" export restraints established outside the discipline of section 201.

Other Publications from the Institute

POLICY ANALYSES IN INTERNATIONAL ECONOMICS SERIES

BOOKS

SPECIAL REPORTS

FORTHCOMING